Bound By Blood

Ψ

S. Connolly

Bound By Blood

Musings of a Daemonolatress

Ψ

S. Connolly

DB PUBLISHING 2014

MMXIV

DB Publishing is an arm of Darkerwood Publishing Group, PO Box 2011, Arvada, CO 80001.

ISBN: **978-1503216365**

Book Design by S. Connolly
Editors: T. Jenkins and W. Hardin
Cover Art by Prism

For those Daemonolaters who find my work inspirational.
You're the ones I write for.

Introduction

I've been writing books about the how-to of Daemonolatry for years. Then recently a dear friend came to me and asked me why I never wrote a book about my views of Daemonolatry, my thoughts on the practice of the arts, and my thinking about modern occult culture (or occulture as a friend of mine calls it). I told her that I did discuss those things - often in fact. The only problem is my views on all of these things were scattered across six years and two blogs, and while easily available, it would require those seeking my views on such matters to sift through six years of blog entries on two websites to find those relevant posts that covered those topics she was searching for. Let's face it — who's got that kind of time? So, inspired, I decided that I would collect all of these blog posts and essays together and see what I had.

If you have followed my blogs, some of these articles may be familiar to you. If you haven't followed, much of this material will be new to you. I've also included three articles that have been included in anthologies for the sake of making them more easily accessible (considering said anthologies are either expensive or sold out). By the time I was done putting it all together it occurred to me that I had enough articles to fill an entire book. So I put it together and handed it over to my editor who, after she read it the first time said this was her favorite of all my Daemonolatry books.

I call it Bound by Blood due to my blood bond with the Daemonic that has spanned thirty years. Possibly longer if you count my Daemonic filled childhood.

I hope you, dear reader, will find my Daemonolatry ramblings interesting, too. Perhaps, in another ten years, I'll publish another collection. So it goes. Please remember as you read that much of this was published in my blog and we've only edited the entries for spelling, grammar, and clarification.

With that I give you *Bound by Blood: Musings of a Daemonolatress (Volume I)*. Enjoy!

BEGINNINGS

The articles in this section of the book discuss getting started in Daemonolatry and my thoughts on beginnings. This is also where I discuss initiation, teaching, and jumping into the fire. Would you like to know more? Read on.

Pre-1990 Paganism and Magick

For those of you new to any pagan or magickal tradition (i.e. you started your path after 1990) I'd like to share some of my observations about how paganism and magick have changed drastically over the last 60-70 years.

Each generation seems to have its own unique take on both magick and religion and I think this younger generation of pagans/magicians (the post-1990 crowd) doesn't really understand how easy they have it nowadays.

I, admittedly, started down my path in 1984 – almost on the cusp of the most recent change in the pagan/magick scene. But I know a good number of people who started in the 60's, 70's and one lady who was practicing back in the 40's. It's amazing the differences each decade brings.

See – it used to be that the occult itself weeded out the dabblers by default. Well – mostly.

Why? Because pre-1985 (before there were thousands of books printed about the subject) books about the occult were not as popular or as easily acquired. Especially in heavily Judeo-Christian areas. This means that unless you lived in a major California city or New York City – you likely had no contact with groups and had little access to books.

Many of us who started out before the information age had to get our information from library books or whatever we could find on the Waldenbooks (one of the big booksellers at the time) bookshelves. This means that we actually had to work harder to find the information we got. Getting your hands on The Witches Bible in 1985 (which was one of the most popular witchcraft texts at the time) was like finding treasured manna. Finding more obscure titles was like hitting a Vegas jackpot. I remember the first time I got my hands on a copy of Goetia. It was one of the best intellectual orgasms of my adolescence.

In many instances — you couldn't get certain books unless you were a member of a certain organization or group. Most organizations/groups wouldn't let you in unless you took classes beforehand. And, sadly, depending where you lived — groups were almost impossible to find. You had to scan advertisements in underground scene newspapers, or hang out at the most prominent local occult shops that could have been 30-100 miles from where you lived. Or you had to know people. A lot of occult stores were mail order only accessible to most. They weren't high quality catalogs either. They were often roughly printed lists of items available – stapled together.

My point being that being an occultist/pagan/magician about 20 + years ago – actually meant you had to do some work to get your supplies, educational materials, and find other like-minded individuals. It wasn't as simple as going to an online social networking site for pagans/magicians – or searching for information in a web browser.

See – nowadays anyone can call themselves an occultist based on "interest" alone. If you post to an occult networking site or have read a few articles — that seems to be enough for one to label themselves a pagan/magician/or occultist these days. Many groups no longer require a person take classes or study before joining a group or taking on a personal label suggesting involvement with a certain tradition.

Back in the day — if you called yourself a pagan/magician/or occultist it often didn't mean you just read about it and socialized with others who read about it. You were often actually doing it. This means you actually stoked a Beltane fire, made a Yule Log, or practiced offering rituals. It also means that you actually practiced magick.

Now – yes, there are exceptions to every rule. Not all old-school magicians were practicing just as not all new school magicians are sitting around "pretending" to be something they're not (though the number of dabblers has increased, I've noticed). I'm also saying that today's magician may not really appreciate that it was the pre-1990 occultists who made it so that all of the post 1990 occultists had easy access to information about occult and magick topics they may not have otherwise had.

It was even worse back in the first part of the 20th century. My friend E told me how back in the 40's you didn't breathe a word about your alternative practices or beliefs to anyone. An open – public journal like this one would have been unheard of. "To keep silent" was one of the most sacred tenants. Getting materials (i.e. books or supplies) was not easy. She also said that she still went to Church on Sundays just to keep everyone from knowing what she really believed or practiced. What a vast difference from today's "My life is an open webpage" philosophy. It's no wonder some of our elders look at the younger generation horrified when they're willing to discuss their beliefs so openly. It's a different world now.

In the 60's – the occult took off in the underground. This, of course, is when Witchcraft came out of the closet and onto the public scene even though the Alexandrian and Gardnerian sects started up at least a decade before. It was also the 60's that birthed LaVeyan Satanism and the Atheist movement he helped mobilize. The 70's seemed to keep what started in the 60's going steady. It was the late 80's before magick, paganism, and the occult experienced another resurgence and growth. That's when all the Llewelyn books started coming out and Weiser titles became more popular. By the time the early 90's rolled around – most bookstores had a healthy smattering of readily available occult reading material. And, of course, once the internet really took off and started invading our homes by 1995 – it wasn't long before there was a thriving online occult cornucopia of reading material and social networking sites. I know this because I was there. I watched this last resurgence in the occult take hold and balloon. I ran the first site on the web for Daemonolaters, which was also popular with the Theistic Satanists — who had no idea there were so many others out there like them.

It also used to be that those of us brought into traditions had real flesh and blood teachers and we respected our elder's experience and what they had to teach us (this doesn't mean we worshiped them or agreed with everything they said — just respected their experience).

Nowadays — everyone who's read one or two books or a smattering of web articles considers him/herself an expert who knows better than those who have been practicing for 20+ years. I'm amazed at the sheer number of folks who think they alone have discovered something no one else in the magickal community has figured out yet. They're usually wrong.

Another marked difference I noticed was in Wicca. Before 1985 — Wicca was very much a religion about being in harmony with nature, and there were rules that allowed for cursing someone else in self-defense. It wasn't until the late 80's when it began morphing into a feminist (with little emphasis on both the male and female – but rather Goddess only), vegetarian only, love, light, and harm none religion. Basically – Christianity with a Goddess at the helm.

Pre-1990 was also back when Witchcraft itself worked in harmony with traditional Satanism (the belief in Satan as a deity), or with Daemonolatry (the worship of Daemons) or any other religion for that matter. And while it still does – this older version of Witchcraft is now referred to as "traditional" witchcraft whereas its modern counterpart is often considered synonymous with the more modern Goddess only light and love Wicca to the under-educated.

I'm kind of sad that things have changed. While I think it's awesome that information is so readily available, I still meet few actual working magicians (i.e. people who actually go beyond arm chair theorism and who actually practice) and few practicing Pagans (people who actually abide their pagan religion more than at the solstices and equinoxes and actually apply the principles their religions teach in everyday life). Most seem to be just playing dress up when it suits them or hanging out with a certain social clique. Being a magician, pagan, or occultist is part of their "image" and social identity rather than a spiritual identity that they take seriously.

Of course I hope I'm wrong and I'm just missing the vast numbers of serious occultists out there.

What We've Lost

Lately I've been looking at Daemonolatry students and it dawned on me that things just aren't the same way they were back in the 80's when I started out. I realized just how much modern students lose now that the master – apprentice relationship between the magus and his/her students only exists for a rare few practicing the arts.

See, not very long ago that's how Daemonolaters learned Daemonic Magick and the practice of Daemonolatry. It was a one-on-one experience. It wasn't necessarily a *group* thing. It was one teacher who had one student and they worked together much like an intern might work at a company specializing in the line of work he wants to go into. Or how an electrician takes on an apprentice and teaches him his trade.

In general – we (and by *we* I'm talking about Daemonolatry specifically) don't do that anymore. Either you're in a group or you're solitary. Some people say solitary is the way to go because of group drama. Others swear by groups. Others still learn from people over the Internet. There are merits to all these methods, but there are missing pieces, too.

Back when I was just starting out we didn't have books about Daemonolatry to learn from so you almost couldn't do it solitary. Sure, you could have had a Daemonic guide and been solitary, but if you wanted the experience of an actual methodology of learning Daemonic magick or Daemonolatry you became an apprentice who studied underneath someone more experienced than you. You were given assignments, as with school, you did said assignments, and you were given verbal or hands on tests. You were also watched over by your teacher as you physically performed the magical exercises. This, of course, required you to be in the same city.

My teacher ran small study groups once a month and I was also at her house every weekend. She was constantly quizzing me and teaching me things just in the conversations we had. She would ask if I'd tried this or that and I would say, "I've never tried that!" Her passion for the subject ignited my own and I happily ran home and tried what she suggested and when we got together for coffee a few days later – we would talk about my work and its results.

You really did the work and got your hands dirty because if you didn't – your teacher would likely drop you in favor of a more worthy apprentice. My teacher actually abandoned a lazy apprentice in favor of me, citing that I was more worth her time because I appeared (in my behavior and actions) to really want to learn, whereas the young man I replaced just wanted to sit around and talk about magick – not actually do it. To make sure I was actually doing the work, my teacher, unbeknownst to me, would give me little tests by asking me pointed questions or inviting me over for ritual and asking me to construct the ritual space with no forewarning or invoke the Daemonic force we were working with that night. She was there to correct me if I made a mistake and guide me when I was uncertain. And like I said earlier – she and I did energy work, meditations, and other magickal exercises together. Sometimes it was just us, sometimes it was in a small study group with others.

I think if you talk to anyone who has had the benefit of having face-to-face conversations with elders or more experienced peers, they'll tell you just how much you learn from that. What you get from that experience can't be gotten by books or even internet conversations. Sure, some of it could come from solitary work, but sometimes to come to things on our own it would take a great deal longer. With teachers as guides, we sometimes come to realizations faster.

Now don't take it as I'm down on solitaries. I'm not. The most spiritual growth you'll likely ever experience will be due to solitary work. I'm also not saying the Daemons themselves aren't good teachers – they are. But it's still not the same thing. I've been an apprentice, I've been in a group, I've been solitary (I am most of the time even now), I've been the student of a Daemonic mentor/teacher, I've had online teachers, so I can attest to the fact that there really is no comparison as all of these methods of learning are distinctly different. I've also been the teacher both in person and online. A magician can get a great deal of experience and education from serving as an apprentice – even for a short time. It often makes for a more well-rounded, interesting magus (imho).

Of course I also realize the sad reality that pairing students and teachers is another ball of wax as it actually requires teachers who are willing to take on apprentices and perhaps that's part of the problem. Not to mention it requires being in the same city.

I have very fond memories of my days as an apprentice. It makes me sad to know how few modern Daemonolatry students will ever have that opportunity.

Coming out of the Broom Closet

Coming out of the broom closet. That's a phrase a lot of pagans and witches use when it comes to telling their families that they're witches and no longer Christian, or whatever brand of religion they formerly practiced (or pretended to practice). I know all about coming out of the broom closet. Been there, done that. Having also been around for a long time I've been witness to a lot of *comings out*, too. While it's hard enough for someone to come out as a Witch or Pagan, it's even worse for Satanists and Daemonolaters. Especially when you have extremely religious relatives of the Evangelical variety. You know the type I'm talking about; the bible thumpers whose initial reaction to the news is to schedule an exorcism or gather the kindling.

I'm also the person a lot of people come to for advice when it comes to *coming out of the broom closet* because some people find themselves in impossible situations. Like they worry that their family and friends will abandon them, or they'll lose their home or job, or that their spouse will divorce them and take the children. All of these things are *valid* concerns when it comes to having *any* alternative-to-Christian belief system. Those of you reading who are members of the GLBT or BDSM communities can also sympathize a great deal, I'm sure. I know all about being *outed* with regard to the latter, too. While sexual orientation and sexual kink are different balls of wax – they share that same element of *difference* and as we know, some people just can't deal with *different.*

Some people with pagan or other-than-Judeo-Christian beliefs prefer to just keep it under wraps. It's easier than dealing with a confrontation. There's only one problem with that. While I don't promote anyone running around shouting their spiritual differences from the rooftops, I do think that in the case of alternative-to-Judeo-Christian spirituality sometimes it's better to just come out of the closet with those close to you. Mind you I'm not saying with everyone, just those people you share the intimate details of your life with whether it's a sister, a child, your spouse, or your best friend.

Sure everyone's situation is unique. If you stand to lose your home, your children, your job or there could be bodily harm involved, then by all means — keep it to yourself. However this doesn't always work. At some point it's very likely that you're going to be *found out* by someone who wasn't supposed to find out. Chaos often ensues.

Those are the e-mails I don't like getting. They often start out, "Help! My [insert loved one here] just found out I was a witch (Daemonolater, Satanist, Magus, etc…) and threatened to [insert punishment for witchcraft here, usually divorce, loss of residence, loss of children, loss of friendship etc...]!"

This usually happens because a family member (or friend) finds a book or an email, a picture, or some other thing that tells them that the person they thought was a God fearing Christian is actually some flavor of pagan, witch or magician and they immediately fly off the handle. That's when you find out how Christian this loved one suddenly is (even if it wasn't evident before) and the ultimatums start rolling out. If you're a teenager or you are living with family or friends or even your spouse you might even get, "You can't practice this or read about this in my house…blah, blah,

blah…"

It sucks.

It happened to me and it's happened to a lot of people I know.

Sure – I know people who have been practicing for years who have somehow managed to keep their religion and practices secret. How I'll never know. But I always wonder for how long. How long before you leave your *Complete Book of Witchcraft*, *Satanic Bible*, *Goetia*, or Crowley's *Magick in Theory and Practice* sitting casually on your coffee table the same day Aunt Martha and Cousin Janet show up unexpectedly for a visit after Sunday mass?

Or you have your family over for dinner one night and decide to let the answering machine pick up only to have the High Priestess of your coven leave a message about the next Full Moon Ritual.

I've known people this has happened to.

Over the years I started telling people to come out to their loved ones as soon as they safely could. Now in some instances it may be in your best interest *not* to tell certain family members. As a matter of fact sometimes leaving grandpa or grandma in the dark is in everyone's best interest. But your spouse — you have to tell them. They need to know. For a good relationship there can't be secrets and if they find out they're going to feel betrayed – even lied to. Then they'll wonder what other secrets you've been keeping.

My husband and I started our relationship with him knowing exactly what I was before we even went out on our first date. Why? Because when I was dating I'd tried it the other way where I kept my religion to myself only to discover that the guy I was dating was a Christian and me being a Daemonolater was the deal-breaker. That is… unless I came back to Jesus. I'm sorry, but my spiritual path was not something *I* was willing to compromise. Not to mention it should never *have to be* something you compromise.

A person who cares about you — truly cares — will love you no matter what your beliefs are. That goes for siblings, parents, spouses, children, friends etc… If that love is conditional (i.e. you better change your religion or I'm divorcing your ass, disowning you, won't be your friend) then I'd re-evaluate that relationship and whether or not it's worth continuing.

Luckily my own experience with coming out happened when I was a teenager. I had enough opportunity to explain my religion to my mother and we have an understanding now. Nowadays she and my siblings collect my Daemonolatry books right alongside my fiction even though they're all happily Christian or Agnostic.

It's certain members of the extended family who have chosen to pray for me and hope my atheist husband and I eventually find God.

Sadly a lot of Christians just don't understand that those of us who have pagan and/or magickal inclinations have them for a reason. We've generally converted from Christianity (or a Judeo-Christian religion) for a reason. It didn't work for us, we explored other options and found something better (for us individually).

So if you're struggling with coming out – know that you're not alone. Oftentimes these things work themselves out. It may take time and a lot of talking. There may be some fighting and tears and all that, but in the end it's worth it to not have to worry about hiding your beliefs or practices as if they're some dirty secret.

It's nice to be able to hang *your* pentagram Yule wreath on *your* front door or leave *your* books out on *your* coffee table in *your* house if people drop by unexpectedly. It's nice to be able to leave your altars up and keep your ritual implements within reach and out in the open instead of hidden in some back bedroom closet. It's nice not having to lie about where you'll be, what you're doing, who your friends are, and who *you* are. Being able to be yourself with those you love will facilitate spiritual growth. Having to lie and hide and sneak around can be stifling. Not to mention it's hard to integrate your spirituality into your life completely when it becomes a separate, secret part of your life.

Leading Horses to Water

One thing I've learned over the years is you really can lead horses to water, but you can't make them drink. This is especially true when it comes to teaching whether you're training someone for a job or apprenticing a student in magick. Sometimes the only thing you can do is share the information and let the other person take that information and use it to accomplish whatever it is they seek to accomplish.

Now in some instances you can actually show someone something, but after that the ball is in their court. They have to be able to take that information and apply it in a meaningful way that helps them accomplish a task or meet their goals.

I experience this a lot with magick. It dawned on me today just how many 101 books (even my own) only scratch a superficial surface when it comes to numerous magickal and spiritual practices. What gives these practices their depth and dimension are the realizations we have when exploring each topic more thoroughly and applying our foundational knowledge to the practice.

When studying Goetia, for example, I came to such a profound realization about certain things that I was literally mind-blown. I honestly thought I had discovered something new since I'd never seen anyone mention it anywhere.

Sydney J. Harris famously said *"Nobody can be so amusingly arrogant as a young man who has just discovered an old idea and thinks it is his own."* Magick is full of moments like this. Of course once you take a step back you realize that this idea is as old as the Gods themselves and other magicians practically spelled it out for you and you were just too ignorant to see what was staring you in the face all along – that self-congratulatory smugness dies a quick death.

My friend Goetic Nick (aptly nicknamed for his extensive work with Goetia) laughed when I shared my revelation. He said, and I have permission to quote him here, "Congratulations. Most people have to have that pointed out to them. That fact that you figured it out on your own speaks volumes."

But this is a perfect example of how a teacher/guide can only lead the horse to water. Some things can only be learned by drinking.

I can tell you to study this or that and that it relates to this or that, but you really need to put the study to practice and see how it all works together first hand in order to come to these realizations yourself. Never will you experience a more sober moment of clarity than that.

It's food for thought.

Initiation

Initiation is an interesting topic. In a lot of groups the process of initiation itself is somehow a way for the group to either pass on their magickal power to the initiate or for the group to help the initiate tap the raw magickal current running through everything by giving them some special key, power, or authority that comes from the group itself. I have a somewhat different perspective of all this even though I came out of an initiatory tradition.

See, my problem with the above is that if this truly is what initiation is, it means that anyone else, at any time, could invalidate your initiation with the simple statement, "Your initiation wasn't done right." or "Your initiation wasn't done by approved persons and therefore it's invalid and you have to start over." There's a lot of power-tripping in telling someone that the only way they can be a true initiate is to have others, also truly initiated by Real (TM) magi, initiate you through XYZ tradition.

In Daemonolatry people go through several types of Rites of Passage. There's baptism, there's initiation, and then there's dedication. The Baptism is the ritual where the practitioner states their intent to begin their life anew in their new spiritual path. The Initiation is basically an introduction (of the practitioner) to the Daemonic Divine and being brought into a group if applicable. In group settings there may even be some light hazing (that's just how it is with our tradition). We believe, however, it's from the Dedication Rite where you actually tap something special, and it's not necessarily magickal current (though that could very well be a part of it) since some people are just spiritual Daemonolaters and don't practice magick at all. The interesting thing about Dedication is that it is not a group ritual and it has to be done by the practitioner and the practitioner alone because it's all about you and your relationship to your divine source. No one — NO ONE can take that dedication ceremony away from you and call it invalid. Sure, people can get kicked out of groups. But when it comes to rites of passage — no one should be able to take away what you gain from a ritual just by telling you it wasn't done right. And truly – YOU are the ONLY one who knows if a ritual was done "right" and if it "took"! Spirituality and magickal work is not about competition, or who's right and who's wrong, or who has more power. It's all about your relationship with your understanding of the divine and your ability to cause change in your world in conformity to your will. Notice how no other human being is directly involved, in a mediator capacity, in that relationship. You don't need a middle man.

So when it comes to initiation I always suggest practitioners, even if they belong to a group, do a self-initiation. That's something between you and all that is. It doesn't involve anyone else. You will know if it "worked" because you'll feel it. It will have a special meaning for you – always. It's a ritual you'll always remember. For a lot of Daemonolaters their Dedication is more powerful a force anyway and this is probably where many of them truly find "Initiation".

I guess I have a problem with authority. I always have. I have never waited for anyone else to give me their "blessing" as it were. The reason being that blessings can just as easily be reversed and can become curses because friendships fade and groups sometimes falter. It's the nature of the beast being the human animals that we are.

I don't need another person to tell me I've been initiated because I know, in my heart and with every fiber of my being that I have been. I know because I can perform effective magick independent of anyone else. This isn't to diminish my teachers or the groups or orders to which I belong. I love you all dearly and I look forward to the ceremonies that celebrate all of us as we reach milestones and goals and each new rite of passage. I've found our study groups and time spent discussing magick and spirituality invaluable, but I still grow in my own light.

I think it's important that magicians remember this. Groups have their place and their usefulness most certainly (as do teachers) – but all of the real work I've ever done, all of the intense growth I've ever experienced, has happened during solitary ritual.

A Process of Initiations

Our spiritual paths are constantly changing to reflect a new understanding or our needs at the time. As a matter-of-fact I contend that it's practically impossible to not change on a regular basis (spiritually-speaking). It's also difficult to remain in a magickal stalemate if you're actually doing the work and practicing.

For those of you who know me, you know that I don't often talk about my magickal work online. Usually because it's personal or I'm in the midst of something and I just haven't sorted my thoughts. None of it is really secret. I don't believe in magickal secrets.

I will happily answer most any question someone poses to me about my magickal practice or my spirituality unless it's so personal that I feel uncomfortable answering. Or if it requires me to break an oath of my Order. I mention oaths for good reason. Read on to learn more.

Yes, I realize some Daemonolatry practitioners (including folks who claim to be generational) choose to keep their journals private or only share selected parts with people and not the whole thing, but that doesn't necessarily mean it's a secret. Sometimes that stuff isn't shared for personal reasons. I, for example, don't share the contents of my *early* journals with anyone outside my group because they're absolutely embarrassing. Teenagers write some pretty silly things in their first magickal journals. It is what it is. However – I do tend to draw a lot from my more recent journals when writing books. So basically I am sharing my information freely (information worth sharing anyway).

Today I'm going to tell you a little bit about the magickal journey I've been on these past few years because it's important to me and I think it will provide readers with some insight into me as a magician, as a person, and as a writer.

While yes, I have taken Oaths to keep certain rituals sacred and within my order, I will happily discuss what these rituals were for, how they manifested and I have no problem sharing "similar" rituals with people simply because I don't think the ritual itself is what manifests results, but rather the intent behind it and the skill of the magician to manifest the desired result. You can get that with a mimic and that's why I included the Caspiel mimic in Infernal Colopatiron.

If you do want the *exact* ritual instructions you would have to gain an invitation to join my order and work through the grades like everyone else. That is the purpose of the oaths. Not to keep information from others (because I'll happily share the information necessary without breaking any Oaths), but to put the magician through a series of steps and tests from initiation to initiation, grade to grade, and to hold those rituals sacred within the Order itself. We all emerge the other end of such rituals differently anyway. If I saw someone with a need for a ritual that I had promised to keep sacred, I would simply write my own version of that ritual and give it to the person in need, telling them to modify it in a way that best suits them and their work. So rest assured there are no *secrets* here, nor am I an Oath breaker. I simply don't believe in magickal secrets. I also firmly believe that only those who understand would know whether or not they had use for a particular ritual anyway. If they didn't, clearly the ritual wouldn't work for them. So if I ever talk about something you find interesting, feel free to ask specific, pointed questions. I encourage it. It's the general questions that annoy me. That's why I write certain books — so I don't have to continually repeat myself. I hate repeating myself (unless I have a point to make).

All of that said – back in December of 2008, I began working toward becoming a more learned, disciplined, and practiced magus. This began with working toward a magician's grade in my Order. The first ritual one must complete after taking a basic Order Initiation is the Path of Ptah – the becoming *as* the creator. This is an interesting step in a magician's growth simply because it requires one to change how one views the self. You must, male or female, come to acknowledge yourself as a creative force. A person who gives birth. I contend this is often easier for women than men since we are often conditioned from birth to perform nurturing, care giving tasks and are often pelted with baby dolls so we can hone our child rearing skills early on. It is, for many females, always expected of us that at some point we will give birth. Clearly males aren't usually conditioned in the same way.

I took two years with this rite. I actually performed the ritual twice. The first time I focused on the end result. The second time I focused on the process. Yes, I realize that's ass-backwards, but it took doing the ritual the first time to realize I hadn't really relished in the process of *becoming* nearly as much as I'd concentrated on what the end result of that *becoming* manifested.

It's funny because the high priest of my Order seemed genuinely surprised to find someone who was willing to take two years to prepare and perform a grade rite twice. Evidently most people give it a month or two prep, then they just do the ritual and move on to the next initiation. What can I say? My parents always told me that anything worth doing was worth doing to the best of your ability the first time. I took my time and I got a great deal out of that rite. I am in no hurry to sprint through the grades just to stroke my ego. I'm in this for the self-edification and I didn't want to cheat myself. Still don't.

I took almost another year to prepare for my LoKIR (Lord of Khemenu Initiatory Rite). It's basically a magician's initiation and introduction to Thoth. I am now at a crossroads. I can choose to take the path of the seer, or the path of the walker. I have to choose my next course of study carefully because this is where I'll be for at least another year or two. I am seriously considering the path of the walker since I've been doing so much work with gate opening and necromancy as of late. Like with anything, however, I want to be sure. If anything I've learned that Thoth is both a strict and patient teacher. When it comes to magick, I've become patient out of necessity. Sometimes we need to just sit and listen to the divine and let our hearts and intuition guide us.

Right now Anpu, Eurynomous, Bune, and Murmur are strong with me. I can feel Seshat and Delepitoré stand aside (for now) as Thoth oversees my education. I always feel the warmth of Leviathan's encouragement. I have decided I will make the decision before the weekend is up.

For context, for the hard polytheists out there, I'm a panentheist (I have, in recent years, rejected the pantheist label simply because it's too small) and I'm soft poly, but then if you're reading this you know this about me, or you should. It does mean that I'm prone to pantheon mixing and if that offends anyone, I am sorry to hear it. But it works for me and I have yet to have a Daemonic force *beat me up* over it. I am also not offended by the term God or any of the names of God, or Christian magick of any kind, since I'm secure in my own beliefs about such things. Basically I don't feel threatened by Abrahamic belief systems since I don't believe in, or buy into, their mythos, and I know where all of their shit comes from. This means I will freely work with Angels as simply another form of Divine Intelligence. Daemon/Daimon (both roots of the word Demon) means Divine Intelligence or Replete with Wisdom, and the longer I work with spirits the more I realize while there may be different types of Divine Intelligence, some bigger than others, they're all still Daimons/Daemons. A rose by any other name... Feel free to disagree.

Foundation

An old friend of mine, we'll call her Stacy, converted from Daemonolatry years ago. She decided it wasn't for her. That's cool. It's not for everyone. So she finally thought she found her path in another occult/magickal based tradition. This time it was an Afro-Caribbean tradition. Well, part of what she didn't like about Daemonolatry (and why she allegedly left) is she felt we were too strict in the way we practiced. Basically, we wouldn't allow her to do just anything and then call it traditional/generational Daemonolatry. That foundational knowledge still needed to be learned (as it is with all magickal practices). So she gets into these other religions and none of the teachers there would take her on. Why? Because again, she didn't want to learn the foundation. She wanted to make up the rules as she went. Learning the foundation and the existing rules (before you run around breaking them) is kind of one of those fundamental things about magick in general.

You can't run around raping other people's traditions by throwing the rules out before you've even learned them. That's not only bad manners, but I wonder if people like this realize that the rules are often there for a reason? Sure – everyone, if they practice long enough, is going to learn the rules on their own. But that's like offering someone a free direct flight (no strings attached) and them saying, "Fuck you! I want to take a 200 mile detour – AND I want to walk to my destination!" I guess it's the individual's choice.

Once you learn the rules and why things are the way they are – you can commence becoming the master by breaking those rules in meaningful ways. This is only logical. Again – I see this as symptomatic of my own generation and the ones after it (in varying degrees). People just don't want to work for anything anymore. They want to read a book and crown themselves "Master Magus Supreme"!

This, of course, leads me back to the training manual I found yesterday. What surprised me is how small the chunks (lessons) are. But back then – these 16 page booklets were studied laboriously and practiced. We literally would spend a month on each booklet with several practice sessions each month. Then, once you mastered a booklet you became tasked with helping those starting that same booklet master it while continuing to your next booklet. And it went on like that for about 10 different booklets and THAT was how you completed your pre-initiate training back in the day. It was hands on.

So much has changed…

The Importance of a Regular Practice

As an author and teacher, I am constantly getting emails filled with questions about Daemonolatry and magick. I don't mind this because I have assistants who help me answer the vast volume of mail I receive. What's interesting is a lot of the questions we get can be answered quite simply, "Establish a regular practice."

- How can I better connect with the Daemonic Divine?

- How can I increase my divination skills?

- How can I learn more about the Daemons or a specific Daemon?

- How can I become closer to my patron/matron?

- How can I advance in my Daemonolatry studies?

- How can I learn ascension?

- How do I get started?

Yes — every last one of these questions has the same answer. Establish a regular practice. Your spirituality is not a weekend hobby or something you simply do when you get off of work at night and/or when you have no other obligations. Your spirituality shouldn't be some separate part of yourself locked away in a closet, only to be taken out, dusted off and used at your convenience. No – it's part of you and you should acknowledge it EVERY DAY.

Now I'm not saying dress in all black or metal concert t-shirts. I am not telling you to wear sixteen of your favorite pentagram-daemonic-sigil-magick pendants at any given time. While the pendants may be symbols and/or reminders of your devotion (as may your manner of dress if you're into that sort of thing), and your talismans manifestations of current magickal works-in-progress. I'm talking about something deeper. This goes beyond the outward aesthetics. After all, many practicing Daemonolaters are consummate professionals who must wear suits or proper business attire during their working day. No, I'm talking about daily PRACTICE.

But, Steph, I don't have time! I'm really busy. I live with non-Daemonolaters.   I hear these excuses a lot. They're JUST EXCUSES to get out of doing anything tangible. Sorry, but developing relationships with Daemons and honing magickal skills can't be done overnight. There are no shortcuts. No magick pills. No magicians or sorcerers you can pay to do it for you.

I think every last person reading this can find fifteen minutes a day for a daily spiritual practice.

Let's take a simple list of items and see what you can do with them, shall we?

- Simple stick incense.

- A simple white tea light candle. Nothing fancy.

- A clay sigil. (Make it out of paper if you want)

- A small finger-bowl with rum in it. (Cups work just as well)

- A prayer cord.

That's it, and a lot of this is optional. For example, if you can't burn incense because you live with someone who is allergic, or who will think you're smoking "the pot", don't burn incense. If you live in a "dry" house – substitute juice or water for the rum. The sigil can be drawn on paper. The tea light can be ANY color. The prayer cord, too, can be any color. All of this can be easily hidden or stowed away and brought out of hiding as needed. Or it could even be left out on a dresser or bedside table and most people wouldn't be any the wiser. Whatever works for you.

So let me explain what I mean by a REGULAR PRACTICE. You wake up, brush your teeth, take a shower, get dressed, have breakfast, and go to work. This is a daily practice. Now I want you to try something.

Tonight – gather all of these items (or what you can get) together and when you wake up tomorrow, brush your teeth, take your shower, then light a candle and incense, offer the wine/rum/water/juice, kiss the sigil, say a prayer with the prayer cord, get dressed, have breakfast, and go to work.

You see what I did there, right? ;) Now – do this for a week. Then try another week. And another.

Tada! It's magick! You've just incorporated a REGULAR DAILY PRACTICE. Simple, right?

Now, take the sigil of any Daemon you wish to work with, and place it under your mattress. Draw it on lined notebook paper if you have to. Whatever works for you. If your nightly routine is undress, brush your teeth, wash up, put on pajamas, go to bed… try this instead. Undress, brush your teeth, wash up, sit on the bed and meditate for ten minutes (even if you're just enjoying the silence), put on your pajamas, go to bed. If you sleep with a partner either do this before they come to bed, or do the meditation in the living room after they've gone to bed. Alternatively you can lay down and do the meditation in the dark right before you go to sleep. No one even needs to know you're doing it.

There you go! You've just added a nightly meditation practice that will enhance your ascension, divination, or magickal pursuits overall. Together you've only added about 15 minutes to your entire daily routine.

The sigil beneath the mattress will help enhance any Daemonic communication through dreams. (Change out the sigil as necessary.)

If you want to take it further and enhance an existing daily practice with additional magickal practice – choose one day a week for a certain type of practice/operation/ritual. For example, I do readings every Thursday and Sunday and have for years. As a result – I get a lot of divination practice and my skills are constantly being used and honed, making me a better reader and seer than I was, say, four years ago. Why? Practice. If you want to work on a certain aspect of yourself or hone your talents for a certain type of magick, add a regular ritual to your weekly routine for a month and see what happens. If you can't keep up with it — try something different.

But DO something and do something EVERY SINGLE DAY even if it's just lighting a candle and acknowledging the Daemonic within. That is how you better connect with the Daemonic or your patron or matron. That's how you develop your magickal skills. That's how you advance, and that's how you get started in Daemonolatry.

Finally, I leave you with words of wisdom from Yoda (because I'm geeky like that): *"Do or do not. There is no try."*

Things Worth Doing

Things worth doing are worth doing right.

This is something a lot of us probably remember our parents or grandparents telling us when we were growing up. Becoming good at something takes time. It takes practice.

Skills for seeing (i.e. divination) are no different. Earlier this week I was approached by a client who was very impressed with my talents. She told me she wanted to learn to speak with the Daemonic Divine like I did. I told her to calm her mind and listen. I also suggested she practice nightly meditation where she said the enn of the Daemon she wanted to speak to while falling asleep to see if she was able to do dream divination. She wrote back several days later saying she'd tried it for two nights and it wasn't working.

I rolled my eyes at first because two nights is really not enough time to give something the good old college try. But I bit my tongue and instead asked her what she was expecting because I often find that when some people think of speaking with Daemons, they're thinking Hollywood sorcery where the Daemon appears, physically, in front of them and starts chatting away (usually in an ominous baritone).

Her response was that she wanted to be able to hear them, just like me. I explained to her that I heard them in my mind's eye. It wasn't like hearing voices, it was a combination of thoughts and words with both visual and auditory cues. It's really hard to explain a mediumship ability to those who don't possess it because I'm not always sure people understand what I mean when I say mind's-eye.

I also asked her how long she'd been practicing. She told me she was my age and had been practicing since her late 20's. She also told me she was an earth sign and she described her daily practice to me which seemed more book reading heavy than actually doing. However, her meditation practice sounded solid.

So I suggested to her it was possible that maybe she just didn't have a talent for it. Or that her expectations were too high. Or that she was grounding herself, which usually happens when you introduce an earthy person to a spirit board. She immediately wrote back and told me that she knew she had an ability because she saw the Daemonic all the time.

I went through and suggested a pendulum and other divination devices that might help her. I also explained gently that it took me a lot of years to get my ability to where it is (28 to be exact).

That's when she wrote back and told me she was giving up. Her approximate 10-12 years of practice became 15 (so I wonder how long she'd really been practicing) and she said she'd tried everything I'd suggested and it just didn't work for her. This is where I started wondering if she was telling the truth. No one works for fifteen years and gets no results. I'm sorry. No one. Not unless you don't have an empathic bone in your body and you're so damn stubborn you don't give up. I think people like that are rare. I think everyone has some ability to some degree, even if it's just a strong gut feeling.

I almost jumped in and asked her if she expected it to happen overnight, which is how she sounded. Obviously something kept her going for so long, otherwise, why would she suddenly give up fifteen years of work after a few failed tries at Dream Divination. My only explanation is that this person hasn't put in the effort and was hoping I had a magick pill, formula, or instant gratification spell that would magickally give her the ability I'd worked 28 years to hone, not to mention I was born with it, so I've had the ability for over 40 years!

Of course that's also when it hit me she might be Clairvoyant, which would explain the lack of Clairaudience and Clairsentience and all the failed attempts at using other divination devices. As a last ditch effort to help this person, even though at this point I was pretty sure she was wanting something fast and easy, I suggested scrying might be her cup of tea. After all, if what she said was true, she sees Daemons far more frequently than most Daemonolaters I know. Actually there's only one Daemonolater I know who sees Daemons that frequently and she has no problems communicating with them whatsoever.

I do not know how my client is doing just yet, but I make a prediction that she shows back up in my email with the complaint that the scrying mirror was a flop, too. After all, three days should do it, right?

Matrons, Patrons, and Mentors - Oh My!

I have known people who made a hasty choice for their Matron/Patron and later redid their dedication to a new Matron/Patron. However, I'm a bit old-school in my personal opinion. Back when I began practicing, we were asked to study and practice at least a year and a day before even considering exploring Matrons or Patrons. I had the benefit of having worked with many Daemons before I made a choice to study Daemonolatry, so I'd already been working with Daemons for about five years already when I went ahead and chose to dedicate myself to Leviathan. I've never regretted that choice and I still feel connected to Him with all of my being, despite the fact that some view Him as no more than a minion of Yam. In my view, He encompasses Yam.

I see no reason to modify or change my Patron and I feel that if one takes his/her time and chooses wisely, (s)he will have no need to change her Patron/Matron either. I don't understand the rush to choose a Patron/Matron. There is no rush, but some insist that they must do a dedication almost immediately. This will almost always lead to regrets later on down the road.

Sometimes when people begin doubting their Patron/Matron choice, it's because they've run across what are known as Mentor Daemons. Or that Daemonic force that steps up to help one with the particular area of path-work that they're in.   For example, while Leviathan is a constant and remains my Patron indefinitely, that doesn't mean I can't work with other Daemons. I went through a period where I did extensive ritual work with Delepitoré. Another period in my life I was very involved with Lucifuge. Another period still I worked with Verrine a great deal. Another point with Ptah, and another point still, Thoth. These periods of mentoring can span years, but eventually these Daemonic forces will step aside as a new one steps up to mentor the practitioner as they enter a new phase in their personal path-work. The beauty of this is that you will get to know many Daemonic forces intimately through this mentoring process and you'll never be working with the same Daemonic forces as your bff. If you find yourself working with the same Daemons as all your friends, consider that maybe you're doing it wrong and worrying too much about your image rather than anything genuine.

Pacts with Daemons – Selling Your Soul in the 21st Century

Perhaps the best, and most culturally known example of the Daemonic pact is from Christopher Marlowe's 1604 play, The Tragical History of Doctor Faustus, which was adapted by Marlowe from the 1592 English translation of The Historie of the Damnable Life, and Deserved Death of Doctor John Faustus, which was originally a chapbook circulating in Northern Germany at the time.

In the play, Faust summons Mephistopheles to gain the knowledge of the devil. Mephistopheles complies and gives Faust magical power and knowledge for a pre-determined amount of time, at the end of which, Faust's soul becomes the property of Mephistopheles and Faust is eternally damned. It always amazes me how deeply ingrained in our culture this story is. Usually when beginning magicians contact me about making pacts with Daemons, it's this type of arrangement they have in mind. "I'll sell my soul to the devil for [insert desire here]."

In addition to this to this, Hollywood has added, to the beginning magician's expectations of 'summoning', the promise of bright flashes of light and flaming pentagrams on the ground from which Daemons arise. Replete with full bodied Daemonic manifestations, of course.

This is problematic for two main reasons: The first is that beginning magicians don't realize the medieval idea of pacting is both fictitious and impractical, and I'll explain why in a moment. Second, it causes the beginning magician to miss the results of magick because said results are not nearly as showy and cinematic as the cultural expectation. That isn't to say magick can't have dramatic results, just that not all magick will manifest in bright flashes of light, Daemonic manifestation, and immediate change. As many longtime magicians will tell you, sometimes the changes are subtle and it's only when we look back that we actually see the transformation in its entirety.   In that respect, hindsight is 20/20.

Another important point is that selling one's soul to the devil and expecting eternal damnation requires one to believe that there is an afterlife and that our soul, the energy or essence of us, escapes mortality with our consciousness intact, and that places like heaven and hell actually exist. The belief in the soul and the afterlife is as varied as the magicians reading this article. My personal belief is we all go back to the source upon death, unless some unresolved issue from the physical realm keeps us tethered to the earthly plane. I contend that for the most part, unearthly spirits like Daemons and such, don't pay much heed to humans themselves unless they're attracted to their light, or if the magician is sitting there waving metaphysical glow sticks and setting down a landing strip laden with all those things that attract certain spirits. But that's my belief based on my personal experiences, and it's perfectly okay if you disagree.

Now let me entertain the reader with the reality that there are no Daemons running amok collecting souls.

In death, if we aren't tethered here for some reason, we all return to that same source beyond the veil, regardless our spiritual affiliation in physical life. The soul is energy. Matter cannot be created or destroyed, it can only change form. Matter is basically a storage unit for energy, and matter can be converted to energy and vice versa. If a Daemon (please know I am using Daemon in the sense of a divine intelligence, the original meaning of the word before Christian perversion), or any other entity for that matter, was collecting souls for use (likely as an energy source), that energy would still exist in one form or another. That's how science works.

We could get into how consciousness works after death, but I do have a limited amount of space here, so let's get back to pacts. Basically, I'm 100% positive there aren't Daemons out there collecting souls for eternal damnation. I contend that heaven and hell, if they exist in any form, are states of physical being that we create for ourselves in the here and now. So if we sell our souls into eternal damnation, we're actually the ones damning ourselves in this physical realm, not Daemons. The Daemonic is generally happy to help out if you simply ask, and respect them enough to actually listen to what they're telling you.

A lot of beginning magicians also erroneously believe that one must make a pact with a Daemon in order to work with the Daemonic. I run across this a lot. In Daemonolatry, initiated Daemonolaters may choose to dedicate themselves to a particular Daemonic force with which they have an affinity, but a dedication is not the same as a pact. Dedication is pledging respect and commitment to a Daemonic force, not necessarily expecting anything in return except maybe the occasional crumb of wisdom, or the connection itself. It's a bonding of sorts. Pacts, on the other hand, are a direct agreement to give something of oneself to another being (physical or not) in exchange for something.

Yes, essentially I'm saying pacts are not a requirement for anyone to work with the Daemonic, however don't take this to mean I don't think pacts aren't useful. On the contrary - pacts can be a very effective form of magick. This is why some people will swear by them. Pacts work on the magician's psychology, and if done properly - can be very powerful. So in the next part of this article I'm going to show you how to make a powerful pact with a Daemonic force, and I'm going to explain how it works.

The first thing one must do is decide what, exactly, one wants. This is not the time to be unspecific. You either want the management promotion with the $120K annual salary with health insurance, bonuses and four weeks of vacation - or you can simply ask for a "better" job and roll the dice. That choice is yours. I've found that being specific gives you more specific results, where as being broad and sweeping tends to work, but not always in the way we expect. Write down what you want and make sure it's really what you want. Do you really want that specific job? Or are you simply wanting the increase in salary and benefits? Or do you really just want to be happy? Be careful what you wish for was an axiom coined by someone who didn't really look before leaping.

Next, decide what you are willing to sacrifice from yourself to yourself in order to make this happen. At this point we're not giving anything to the Daemonic. Instead, you may need to sacrifice time or put in more effort to get what you want. Basically - how bad do you want it and what are you willing to do? You get out of something what you put into it. Lack of effort often results in lack of success.

Third, find a corresponding Daemonic force to work with. My personal choice in any type of monetary/job magick is Belphegore. However, Belphegore is best fed with the magician's blood, and this may not work for everyone. Belial might be a tamer choice for those who don't want to sacrifice a few drops of their blood for what they want since he's perfectly happy with offerings of plants.

Then you'll need to decide what you want from the Daemon. At this point I suggest the magician evaluate his expectations. If you're seeking to have it handed to you on a silver platter with no effort on your part, expect the magick manifest in unexpected ways. It will work, yes, you just may not be pleased with the result. Instead of viewing the Daemonic as genii who will grant you three wishes, I always recommend looking at the Daemonic as your support staff. Your support staff gives you the information you need to make informed decisions, presents you with opportunities, and helps you find whatever it is you need to manifest the results you want, whether it's a tool, a relationship, an attitude, or an emotion.

The more we begin to realize that magick really is about helping ourselves by knowing ourselves and by doing things to better ourselves, the more successful the results. This is definitely the case when it comes to pacts because pacts really are more about ourselves than the Daemonic. The Daemonic is simply the support staff that we "hire" to help make it happen. The pact you make is, ultimately, with yourself and your determination and willpower. The Daemonic force is holding YOU accountable to yourself.

So a pact may read something like this (if you're being rather unspecific, and in the case of soul-mates I do recommend being unspecific when it comes to name names of potential partners):

For the great Asmodeus I, [name], offer three drops of my blood in exchange for knowledge and opportunity to help me find my soul mate. Herewith I affix my seal.

You may choose to add qualities of the person you're looking for into the pact. You may write it with far more elegance than the above. Write it up however you wish. Just make sure you put the Daemons name, your name, what you're offering specifically in exchange for what specifically. After you write this out on parchment using a magickal ink attuned to your intent, you would begin your ritual, invoke the Daemonic force you're seeking out, and then read your pact aloud to the Daemon to solidify your intent. To this -

you would sign your name in the presence of the Daemon and, in this instance, add a few drops of your blood. Then the parchment is burned in the offering bowl, turning matter to energy, and symbolically, alchemically transforming the request from a heart-felt want to pure intent. From there - it will become reality.

In this example, Asmodeus is not going to drop a soul-mate off on your doorstep with a quick, "Here you go! Enjoy!"

Nor is He going to hand over the person you asked for by name, because that means influencing the other person, perhaps against their will. This often turns out badly. If you've ever had a stalker you know exactly what I mean.

However, Asmodeus may direct your attention to a party at a friend's this weekend and suggest you go. He may suggest you give yourself a shave, or direct you to toward a certain part of the room while you're there. And there you may meet someone who laughs at your jokes and shares your interests, leading to the opportunity of a date. If you ultimately just wanted sex, perhaps this person goes home with you. Asmodeus, in this example, merely provided the information and opportunity. You made the ultimate choice to act on the opportunity by attending the party and you made a choice to talk to the other person and ask them out. (This is a very simple example, don't expect all encounters will happen this way.)

Now on to the questions you probably have about now.

Is three drops of blood enough? Yes. In Daemonolatry we have a saying: The blood is the life. (Praise be Sobek.) You are willing to sacrifice your OWN blood for what you want, and that says a lot. Psychologically this suggests you are serious enough to suffer some pain (even if it is small) for what you want. Not to mention blood is very sacred. It's your essence, your very life-force. Without it, you would not exist. We carry within us the blood of our mothers, their mothers, and the blood of our entire ancestry. Never underestimate the power a single drop of blood holds. It's not the quantity that counts. It's the intent behind it.

Why not just kill an animal and use their blood? In that case you're not the one suffering or losing your life for what you want. I find that killing an animal for no other reason than for its blood rather cowardly. Unless you plan on eating the cooked animal flesh afterward, it's not a respectful sacrifice. Some may disagree with me and that's their right. I simply see no reason to practice animal sacrifice unless the animal is thanked, you kill it humanely and then use its flesh for sustenance afterward. This means that animals we normally consider food are fair game, but neighborhood cats, dogs and even small rodents are off limits. Don't be unnecessarily cruel because it will come back to you in spades.

Why not my soul? Well, I suppose if you must, you can sell your soul. I just personally find the idea trite. Not to mention you can, theoretically, only sell your soul once. So you better make it a good pact if you're going with the soul-selling angle.

What other things can I sacrifice? Plants always work, but I think the best ones are those that you've grown yourself. Or wine you've made yourself. Something that you've put something into. Whatever you sacrifice, it has to mean something to you and in the case of non-blood sacrifice, it should be something you've put effort in.

What if my pact doesn't manifest? All pacts manifest, they just don't always manifest in the way we want or expect. Just like all magick works, it may just not work how you want it to. Or - you may be expecting results that are unrealistic, or the expected results and the real results aren't coinciding. Some results may also take longer to manifest. If, in six months, you didn't get any results whatsoever, that may be a sign that you need to re-evaluate your true intent. After all, most of us really have no genuine desire to be famous millionaires. We simply want to be happy, surrounded by people who love us, and to have enough so we don't have to worry about the month-to-month bills. If you really had a strong enough desire to be a millionaire, you would be.

What happens if I break my pact with the Daemon? Depends which part you break. If you don't offer up what you said you would, the Daemon may simply ignore you and go on its way. If you do offer up blood or whatnot, but refuse to listen to what the Daemon is trying to tell you, or you ignore the opportunities you're presented, the Daemon may simply stop trying to help, ignore you, and go on its way. Now if you've offered something up that is non-refundable, souls, first-born, things like that, psychologically that could do some damage. Depends how superstitious and afraid of your own shadow you are. Or how prone to emotional discord you are. Each person's results will be different based on mental stability and personal fears. Of course ultimately if you break your pact the person you cheat is yourself, and that's punishment enough because no one can ever be as hard on us as we often are on ourselves.

So if everything you say is true, why magick, why pact-making at all??? Some people need ritual to set their minds to something. Some people need a way to focus their intent, and performing rituals, magick, and working with spirits helps to that end. The mind is a very powerful thing. Add to that coinciding energy in the form of spirits, plants, stones, color etc... you create a force to be reckoned with. The Daemon and all the tools and elements of magick are simply supportive. They draw things and opportunities to you, allow you to attune yourself to the proper energy for affecting change, and help you put your mind and effort toward what you really want. That isn't to say there is or isn't a "supernatural" element to magick, just that for best results, add the power of the human mind. Don't forget the Hermetic axiom: The universe is mental. We do create our own realities, magick, including pacts, just make it a little easier.

Sometimes It Chooses Us

I thought today I'd do a little soul baring and tell you about something that happened to me this week.

Now mind you my intention in sharing this story is not to "climb upon the cross", but rather to share an interesting milestone in my own spiritual path.

So several months ago I went to my OTH (Ordo Templi Hekau) temple priest and asked him if we could strike the "Lector" off of my "title" in the group because the truth is I've never wanted to be a teacher. I'm kind of bitchy and I have no patience whatsoever. If I do teach, it's through my books. The temple priest told me no. No explanation, no discussion, just no. I was kind of pissed off about it at first because I had done my share of teaching to meet the requirements of the degree and position I was working toward, and through all of it I learned that I just don't like teaching.

Then last month I completed my LoKIR (Lord of Khemenu Initiatory Rite) and placed myself in service of Tahuti, Seshat, and Delepitorae (pardon my non-standard spelling) and took on the role of Sesh (i.e. scribe) in our temple. It seemed after this happened that suddenly I began having more Daemonolatry traffic than usual in my mailbox and in my reading and working requests.

Over this past weekend, after a particularly hectic week filled with many Daemonolatry to-do's I complained to a fellow OTH member how overwhelmed I felt. That's when she gently reminded me that this was, in fact, the job I signed up for. I was now in service to the Daemons of magick and knowledge and part of that job is to use my talents to help others. She also pointed out that no matter how much I fought it, I would always be teacher whether I wanted to be one or not, just as I would always be sought after to help others due to certain talents.

You know how sometimes when you knew something all along but you were either in denial or you didn't think much of it and then that 2×4 of reality comes back and smacks you upside the head, really driving the point home? That's exactly what happened to me. For the first time in 28 years I finally feel like I really "get" what it means to be in service to the Daemonic and other Daemonolaters — not just myself.

Sometimes, as a priest, that sacrificial offering that you make on behalf of others is yourself.

And when this realization hit me I thought, I'll be damned. So it is.

It's an interesting contemplation and I thought I would share it.

Sure, several other revelations followed, but this was, by far, the most profound one and I have to admit, it's much more interesting blogging fodder, for me anyway, than ritual atmosphere.

Discrimination & Discernment

This article is a reprint from S. Connolly's personal blog dated June 14, 2011. It has been moderately edited for inclusion here.

An acquaintance recently posed the question, "How important is discrimination on a magical and spiritual path? And ... how often is discrimination ignored because of a feeling that one should be more "accepting" of others?" It's a brilliant question actually.

So many people use the word discrimination to suggest unfair treatment, when in fact the actual definition of discrimination (aside from making a distinction for or against someone based on something other than individual merit) is making fine distinctions or judgments. Discernment means an acuteness of judgment or understanding. It can also mean to have discriminating taste (i.e. fine distinctions).

In a group, discrimination can be a wise thing. Without any discrimination (as in making fine distinctions) you can open yourself up to a world of hurt. This goes for everything – not just magickal or religious communities, but also when choosing friends, jobs, a home, etc... as not everything or everyone is unfairly judged.

You wouldn't buy a house with a heaving foundation, would you? Or take a job that paid you less than minimum wage? Would you choose to take art classes from a teacher who couldn't paint or draw? Then why should you choose to allow people into your life who might be bad for you – spiritually or otherwise?

One example is that many occult group leaders learn the hard way that one must discriminate against those with alcohol or substance abuse problems. Why? Because people like that can wreak havoc on a group or take down other people with them when they start toppling over the edge.

You might be wondering to yourself, "But shouldn't their spiritual/religious organization help them?"

To the extent that they give them the phone number to a substance abuse hotline – yes. But otherwise the answer there is likely no because the fact of the matter is that in non-mainstream religions (and sometimes even in larger mainstream religions) the clergy or leadership isn't trained well enough to help a person who has a substance abuse problem. That requires professional help. The same goes with un-managed mental disorders.

It's not a magickal or spiritual order's job to "fix" broken people. If a person is broken they need to seek professional help. Not to mention a huge part of fixing themselves is about taking self-responsibility and doing the self-work to fix themselves. Anyone joining a religion or magickal order to get "fixed" by someone else, or by the gods/Daemons, is in for a rude awakening.

It is a group leader's discrimination that can help weed out those people who are looking for a quick fix and looking for other people to fix them. You have undoubtedly met people over the years who have bashed their religion because they didn't "grow", "learn", or "get fixed" by it (or by the other people involved in it). Well – that's likely because they didn't do the work. Any spiritual path can help a person grow, learn, and change as long as they do the self-work required to help themselves, instead of waiting for someone else to do it for them. A priest (or an adept) is merely a guide – not a miracle worker. The old adage "You can lead a horse to water but you can't make him drink" comes to mind. (See earlier article.)

You may also find yourself *for* discrimination when it is clear that a certain person isn't a good match for your group or after 10+ years of practicing a religion/spiritual path or belonging to a magickal order they still need hand-holding. The latter is usually a sign that they're stagnated and aren't growing.

It's perfectly fair to not put an unstable person in a leadership position where they're tasked with helping others find foundation in their lives. It's equally fair for magickal students to look at their teachers with scrutiny and pick teachers based on stability. Seriously – if a teacher doesn't have their own life together, should they be teaching others how to get their lives together? It's a fair question.

If you want all out acceptance and plenty of sympathy and attention regardless – join a Judeo-Christian faith. A big impersonal church can handle all kinds of different personalities. A small group may not be able to do the same thing. Like it or not – humans are social creatures. Humans are very clique-y by their very nature (despite how many people scream about wanting to be individuals). Most people want to feel a sense of belonging or have a place where they feel they fit in. If you join a group started by three friends, don't expect to walk in, march up to the pulpit and start making demands that one of the friends is booted from the inner circle just because you don't like them. The sad truth is that unless the friend is doing something the entire group dislikes – that person is staying right where they are and you're probably going to be the one who gets booted (unless you get pissed off and leave). On that same token – you might end up hitting it off with the inner circle and they may discriminate in your favor – deciding you'd be a good leader and tasking you with some group responsibility.

Is it fair? Probably not. But that's human nature, that's how it works. Life isn't fair. Humans discriminate all the time and in seemingly unfair ways.

Discrimination is also beneficial in cases where a member (or leader for that matter) is excessively antagonistic and is consistently creating drama within a group. This can destroy a functioning group. That's why there needs to be some discernment and discrimination when adding people to a group, or removing someone. Many of us have admittedly discriminated against potential members who seemed overly needy. In a group where no one has time to hand-hold – it's only fair to the needy person that you don't accept them into the group or you remove them from the group. The reason being that they're not going to get what they want or need from group membership and their neediness may feel like a burden to group members, making more than just one person unhappy. It's a waste of time for everyone.

Sadly it can take these people years to realize you were right in removing them from your order or group. Sometimes there's no easy way to get this to happen. Sometimes it can require a group leader kick someone out of his/her life (and/or their group) knowing everyone will be better off for it down the road. These decisions should be weighed carefully and done as tactfully and gently as possible.

The same could be said for friendships or business associates. Relationships need to be mutually beneficial for them to be healthy and to thrive. A relationship should end once it's clear one party needs more than the other can provide. Or when only one person is giving and another is just taking (and taking and taking). Or when you notice one person isn't growing in the relationship and the relationship itself is causing one of the parties to stagnate. Perhaps this is an over-simplification, but it's the general gist. This is true for all things in life.

Is it fair? Again - probably not. But then life isn't fair

and it never will be.

If you are the person being removed from the group, try being accepting about moving on once a relationship has ended. If you are discriminated against by a magickal order or religious group – don't look at it as a bad thing. It's probably a blessing and you just haven't realized it yet. You wouldn't have been happy there anyway (and it probably wouldn't have been a positive growth experience) and this way – you can keep searching for a group or community that IS right for you. And if you're on the other end of that and have to be the person who is discriminating – don't feel guilty for it. Being accepting of everyone can cause a great deal of grief. Allowing someone who was a convicted pedophile into a group with children is probably not a good idea. Letting completely unstable people sit at the head of your group and lead others is probably not a good idea.

The needs of the many sometimes outweigh the needs of the one (or few) and as a group leader it's your job to keep the group together and functioning in the way beneficial to the most people. Not always an easy task since at least one person (the one who is a problem) and his/her supporters is bound to be hurt by your decision and go off on a rampage against your group. Such is life if you want harmony and stability – especially in a magickal or esoteric order.

Please be reminded that we're not talking about age discrimination, sex discrimination, sexual orientation discrimination, or any other type of discrimination based on someone's personal preferences that would have nothing to do with a person's interactions with others in the group. None of that should have bearing on someone's membership in a group at all and the GenDem Group as well as TG Daemonolatry is a very inclusive community when it comes to sexual orientation, ethnicity, gender, and age. We're talking about discrimination based on well intentioned, reasonable expectations of group members based on the existing group and its dynamic.

A good test to see if someone fits with your group is to ask yourself the following questions:

1.   Does the person represent your group?

2.   Does the person need more than the group can give?

3.   Does the person's mental or addiction problems affect the group?

4.   If your group is not a teaching group, is the new person at the same place spiritually as others in the group?

5.   Can everyone get along?

6.   Is your decision to discriminate fair to the majority?

Your answers to these questions should tell you whether or not you're making a fine distinction or if you might want to re-evaluate your choices.

As always, reason and good judgment in leadership will take a group far.

IMAGE

Aside from my involvement with Ordo Flammeus Serpens, the Gen Dem Group, and Temple Thoth Seshat, I am still primarily a solitary practitioner. So much of people's occult involvement these days centers around social groups, social media, and social image. However, image is only skin deep. A friend of mine calls occult culture like this "occulture". I like this word. It sums up the social aspect of the occult world rather perfectly in my opinion. Just remember that I call it like I see it, and sadly, I'm misanthropic toward the greater "occulture" for a reason. The following essays and articles address several points of the greater Daemonolatry and Magickal "occulture" and my views therein.

A Magickal Spiritual Life

Spirituality is not something that can be so easily disconnected from living life itself. So when one asks if my practice is more spiritual vs. more magickal, I often reply that life itself is both spiritual and magickal. Neither of these things can be separated out of my life. Nor would I want them to be.

I find magick in the night sky. I find a good rain storm spiritually uplifting. Even walking through my garden becomes a mystical experience when I tend the magickal plants growing in it. Yesterday, for example, I picked several sprigs of mint. Some of it to dry for an incense I'm making, and some to re-pot in the greenhouse. When I'm cleaning my floors I view it as an opportunity to engage in moving meditation, making the simple act of doing domestic chores a spiritual exercise. When I cook I find myself weaving magick into whatever I'm making to bring good health and prosperity to those eating it.

Spirituality and Magick are not weekend hobbies. They're not something you put on Friday night before going out with your friends or take off Monday morning before heading to your boring office job. Spirituality and magick are, or should be, inseparable parts of us that are experienced daily in just about every task we undertake. The easiest way to realize this is to be mindful of what you're doing day-today and how it impacts your spiritual and magickal life. Everything we do from recreation to work, to bathing impacts our well-being and our spiritual health and how we perceive our magickal practice.

Yes, I imagine this doesn't sound evil or scary enough for those who are primarily "image occultists", but then my magickal and spiritual practice is not a fashion accessory. It's who I am and it permeates every part of my life.

In what seemingly unrelated day-to-day activities have YOU found spiritual nourishment or magickal inspiration?

Daemonolatry Organizations and Their (In)Significance

Okay, maybe I'm being a bit unfair with the title of this post. Daemonolatry Organizations aren't insignificant, but they are greatly misunderstood. People seem to think they're like other occult orgs out there like Temple of Set, Golden Dawn (if I say GD in my posts, please know I often mean GenDem instead of Golden Dawn, I apologize for any confusion this has caused or may have caused in the past), or OTO.

The reality is they're not quite the same thing. First – there is currently no such thing as an "online" Daemonolatry organization. In this I mean we don't have an online church or group with a degree system or course of study that just anyone can belong to. At most, we have an org sponsored website for practicing Daemonolaters regardless their group affiliation. On this site we have volunteer adepts and clergy who offer classes. Sometimes they're free - sometimes not.

Second – all of the Daemonolatry organizations I know of do NOT recruit membership, nor are they actively seeking members. For a lot of groups, you have to be local to be considered for membership. Oftentimes membership is at the discretion of the group.

Third – Most (not all) Daemonolatry organizations

are merely groups whose members get together to socialize and worship. We're not like some occult orgs where the entire purpose is teaching students the magickal arts or getting together to work magick. This doesn't mean there aren't magickal Daemonolatry organizations out there or that none of them are encouraging their members to embark on The Great Work, there are, but they work much the same way. You can express your interest to join, but they will pick and choose who they will accept in.

Is this elitist? If having standards for membership is elitist, then yes. But you also have to remember that we don't have the same kind of crazy ass drama a lot of occult organizations do, and this is why we don't.   Yes, all groups are going to have a conflict here or there (put any more than one person in a room together and eventually there is going to be some conflict since not everyone is going to agree with everyone else 100% of the time) but we don't have nearly the drama some other occult organizations have.   When we do have drama, it is usually due to one trouble maker who is new to a group anyway.

Besides – groups are overrated. Most people don't realize, when they write to me to inquire about OFS, that first, we not a TYPE of Daemonolatry. Second, they don't realize that we're a real-world group specific to a specific city. We're not national or international. Finally, they don't seem to realize we're an organization for WORSHIP and socialization specifically. Yes, sometimes we get together and talk Daemonic magick, but that was never the purpose of the group. We're also not a teaching group (not all groups are). If we bring noobs into the group, the most they can hope for is some of us to offer a reading list and to answer questions. After all – a lot of magickal work is best suited to the individual on a solitary basis anyway.

About this time someone always chimes in, "But to learn Traditional GenDem type practices and inner-circle, inner-sanctum or advanced stuff you have to be in a group!"

For some stuff, yes. But it's stuff that would only be of interest to specific people anyway. I often think people are looking for some secret knowledge or something.

Don't get me wrong – if you want to join a group for the right reason that's one thing. But there are a lot of wrong reasons, too.

I've noticed that nowadays some of the big draws to group membership include:

• Titles (for the alleged prestige they have – everyone wants to be a priest)
• Secret Knowledge (usually so they can brag about it to someone else)
• Image (for some people keeping up the social image of being an occultist is key, not to mention all the cool kids are doing it.)

Some of the right reasons for group membership include:

• Personal edification and spiritual growth.
• Commiseration with others of the same faith.
• Sense of community.

But alas, the latter three are best suited to local groups or orgs where you can physically interact with the people and talk face-to-face, and it's unlikely you'll be able to find such a group on the Internet unless you are lucky enough to be invited to a private video-chat group (yes, they do exist).

Just remember that you don't need a group to

practice Daemonolatry and if you don't have a local group it doesn't mean you can't start one.

Sexism in Magick

I'd like to address an interesting phenomena that's been bugging me as of late. And no – don't take this post as me whining or screaming discrimination. I'm not. I'm just shedding light on something that exists and a lot of people don't talk about.

In general and overall – I'd say there's very little sexism (if any) among enlightened magicians. I generally don't run into sexism at all. Because of this, imagine my surprise and shock when I do encounter it. Make no mistake about it, folks. Sexism among magicians (more specifically grimoiric and ceremonial magicians) is alive and well despite its rarity. Now of course no one comes out and says, "Magick is a man's domain, no women allowed" in such a direct way since that's politically incorrect these days, but that's essentially what I've been told by two different men in the past two years.

As a matter of fact, one man was a fan of my books until he discovered I was a woman. I got an e-mail, "You're a woman?" When I replied yes, a barrage of insults and criticisms followed.

Another male had the audacity to "poo-poo" all my books on the subject of magick (Daemonolatry Goetia to be more precise) and tell me that he was looking forward to reading my fiction, because it most likely suited me better.

No- he never poo-poo'ed any of the male authors on the subject of Goetia. Didn't go after Michael Ford and his take on a Luciferian Goetia. Never went after any of the male authors in OTO, Poke Runyon, or the infamous Steve Savedow about their perspectives of Goetia. No- he specifically had a bone to pick with me and the Daemonolatry Goetia. And was quick to point out that I was a "she" as he dressed me down for my untraditional viewpoint and practice of Goetic Magick.

I've even had a well-known female British author approach me and tell me how unusual it is to run across a woman who practices Goetia.

Now I know back-in-the-day magick was a male-only pursuit (unless you were talking about folk magick/witchcraft), but times have clearly changed. Sure, there may not be as many women working Goetic magick out there, but we are here and our voices, views, and perspectives of such magick are no more invalid than a males. We women work grimoiric magick, too. And Enochian. Funny how these same men who have a problem with my views don't seem to get all ass hurt when a male comes out with unconventional views about said long standing magickal practice within ceremonial magick or grimoiric magick. But if a woman does it – holy shit — it's the apocalypse!

Or is it that I really am that controversial and my views are really that far out in left field? LOL! Doubtful. I've read far more controversial work than my own.

I wish I understood the reasoning behind this sexism when it comes to magick, but the only things I can think of is the men who feel this way must either A. hate women, B. have feelings of inadequacy as magicians, C. really believe women have no place practicing magick, D. see a woman as an easy target for their venom and know-it-all stance on the magickal arts (and they're too chicken-shit to pick fights with male magicians who hold similar unconventional views).

So to those two gentlemen who seem to stalk me on the Internet — sure, criticize my work and disagree with my views and practices. That's fine. But don't attack me as a person and call me completely ignorant while singing the praises of (and not equally criticizing) the male authors out there who hold very similar views to mine on the same topics. Because then it just makes you look very sexist. Just sayin'…

Contemplate This on the Tree of Woe

"Contemplate this on the tree of woe." – Thulsa Doom (Conan the Barbarian)

Hmm. What shall we contemplate today? Today I'm actually contemplating labels and how restrictive they are. Everyone is always trying to attach their own definition to subjective self-labels in such a way that it excludes some and includes others based on personal viewpoint (and who we get along with – or not). This makes me wary of labels and makes me want to define myself in broad, sweeping terms, or by usage of such exact or unique labels so that first, no one will misunderstand, but second so people don't think they know me (when they don't) and third so no one can tell me I must be a certain way to fit the parameter of a certain label. This happens a lot with religion. It also happens in political affiliations and even within specific groups. I don't have time to fight over labels, one-true-ways, or whatnot. I'm too busy living life to give a crap really. 500 different people with 500 different beliefs could all label themselves Satanists and I could give two craps about the differences between them – let alone what makes them more "real" or "authentic" than the next guy. Good for you – you're all Satanists. I have no challenge to that. Don't care. I am technically not a Satanist by my personal labeling system (even though some will insist I am while others will agree with me and tell me I'm not...)

Next contemplation. I am very annoyed by how some people define words. First – you can't make up definitions for words. We already have books of agreed upon meanings for words. We call them dictionaries. Sure, we can assume implication of a word based on our own experience, but this tends to make our interpretations of such things both dubious and subjective at best. When I say I worship the Daemonic Divine, for example, I don't mean I grovel before my deity as an unworthy inferior. Worship actually means to hold in high regard and have respect for. It is the context in which some religious folks put worship (as an unworthy inferior being waiting for deity to throw them a bone) that causes so many people to find an aversion toward worship in the first place. Just as the word hope does not imply lack of conviction or uncertainty, but rather realism. If you live your life stating nothing but absolutes and the exact opposite happens you're going to be far more disappointed than the guy who, for example, throws his invention out to the world hoping it will do well. Expecting it to do well and then having it flop — that's usually enough to discourage most people from trying something like that again. But throwing a project out into the world and hoping it does well is more realistic and less painful if it does flop. It also isn't nearly as discouraging and will often encourage the person to go back to the drawing board and try again. Hope simply means (and this is a direct quote from dictionary.com) "the feeling that what is wanted can be had or that events will turn out for the best." Nothing wrong with having hope. It does not make one weak or indecisive to have hope. Nor does it make one weak to worship something (especially when that something is also a part of the self).

Final contemplation for today – anger is not a weakness nor is it a bad thing or a negative thing. That's one of the biggest misconceptions out there. It's a very Christian idea to think Anger is an emotion we should ignore or suppress at all costs. Anger is motivating. It can change us.

We can channel our anger into productivity (that's what I often do) and we can use it to motivate action toward change for the better. After all – without anger the Civil Rights movement wouldn't have happened. The Civil War would have never happened. People wouldn't have left their homelands to move to the United States in search of a better life for themselves or their families. There are so many positive things that have come out of Anger. Anger is only bad for those who don't know how to take coal and transform it into gold. This might be where alchemy comes in handy. Regardless, there is no black and white. Only shades of gray. Once you learn to see the good in the bad and the bad in the good – the lines blur and that black and white worldview disappears. I find it freeing. Not everyone does. Some people need black and white otherwise the world doesn't make sense to them. I prefer to see it through Hermetic eyes. "All things are the same, just different degrees of the same."

Perceptions of Light and Dark

I recently read a blog by a witch who was annoyed that some people think all witches are wiccans and that all witches are "fluffy bunnies". Along with a discussion about religious balance. Then, of course, she began discussing "darkness".

I feel about the terms "light" and "dark" the same way others feel about fluffy bunnies.

See, light and dark are perceptions and for whatever reason - a lot of people are absolutely fixated on light and dark.

Even I began my path enamored with the darkness. I've always been an explorer like that. I think that's almost a prerequisite for choosing a "dark" spiritual path to begin with.

But here's the thing about "darkness". When you spend your entire life looking into every nook and cranny and jumping into every dark crevice you can find, your perception of what's dark changes. After all, once you've explored the dark you've shed light on it and it's no longer hidden or unknown. Therefore, for you, it stops being dark.

Authenticity

I want to take a moment to discuss paganism, occultism, spirituality and authenticity. People LOVE debating and questioning the authenticity of anyone who doesn't believe, practice, or grow spiritually in the same way they do. I think anyone who thinks their way is the only way or the only one-true way of anything (with regard to spirituality) and believes that their particular way is the only way for everyone – is delusional. Personal spiritual paths may be right for individuals, but spirituality is not one-size-fits-all. Sorry. It isn't.

One of my friends posted on Facebook her frustration with, in particular, Reconstructionist pagans who look down their noses at polytheists who don't practice their religion with any historical accuracy. My view on that is this: I've always viewed the Daemonic (and Gods) as progressive and not static. So in my not-so-humble opinion the Daemons (or Gods and Goddesses) don't require we work with them (or worship them as the case may be) in the same way our ancestors might have. They require us to work with them in the way most beneficial to us NOW so that they can impart the wisdom and lessons they have for us NOW. I think this is where the whole Hellenistic, Khemetic, Canaanite, Celtic and Sumerian Reconstructionist movement(s) and the modern Daemonolatry movement differ a great deal

I think getting lost in the details and snubbing those who don't is just an excuse to not face the fact that one's religion/spirituality is really between themselves and the divine. The details don't necessarily matter (not in the grand scheme of things anyway). You either use your spirituality to grow, face your physical and mental self, and find your place among all that is – or you do everything you can to run away from that kind of intimacy and self- knowledge. Getting lost in details is a great way to run from self-work. Just my opinion.

One of my biggest issues with the modern occultist and pagan movements in general is that in a lot of ways it reminds me of the SCA (to which I used to belong many years ago), but for people with alternative beliefs and practices. It's like a part-time fantasy world people escape to on the weekend where their fancy titles and snubbing those who don't acknowledge their fancy titles is how they make themselves feel better about their dreary, boring twenty-first century lives. It makes them feel important – like they're doing something or making a difference.

Now contrary to how it might sound – I am not against this – not at all! Life can be boring. We all need hobbies. A little fantasy can be healthy (in moderation). I also think people should toot their own horns, pat themselves on the back, and try to boost their own self-esteem by declaring they are, too, divine. I just have no intention of willingly allowing myself to be fodder for someone else's low self-esteem, and far too many pagans, occultists etc… do allow it IMO. When you engage in arguments of who's authentic and who isn't – it's all about egos. It's counterproductive to self-growth and it serves no genuine purpose except to temporarily boost a low self-esteem.

I also don't begrudge anyone's love for history, just know that people like that remind many of us of civil war Reconstructionists (thanks to Sharon for that analogy). Yeah – they may be reconstructing the civil war (based on a biased

21st century viewpoint and modern sensibility) but no one's dying (i.e. – still not realistic because the participants don't hold the same worldview or come at the events from the same emotional place). Just remember that. ::wink:: If you really want to reconstruct a temple to Artemis – you better be practicing blood sacrifice (of deer I believe it was, correct me if I'm wrong) if you want me to take that seriously and not laugh at you when you lament how other pagans are not as "authentic" as you. If you're a magician who can recite Agrippa forward and backward but you've never performed a ritual because you lacked the "authentic" ingredients – don't expect me to not laugh at you when you lament how other magicians and occultists are not as authentic as you.

To me – authenticity is about what you believe and what you do when you're not talking about reconstructing the religion (or theorizing about the magick). How you live life OUTSIDE your weekend social gatherings with other Reconstructionists, occultists, pagans or whatever. Do you just talk the talk – or do you walk the walk? Are you just a weekend occultist/pagan or whatever? Is it just a social clique or an image you're trying to portray? Authenticity is about living your spiritual beliefs 24/7 or practicing magick without an audience. Not just lamenting about your beliefs or practices online on forums, Facebook, or whatever social networking site or blog you post ideas to. Do you have a relationship with your deities when no one else is around? Do you give offerings without having to announce it to someone every time you do? Are you embarking on the Great Work without needing a human cheer-leading squad and audience?

If the answer is yes, then in my opinion you're authentic no matter what your beliefs or spiritual path is. Everything else is moot.

Fluffy

Okay, maybe a little. I like fluffy kittens and soft puppies. I'm a sucker for fluffy bunnies, too. They're so adorable with their flippity-flop ears and foofball tails. Who doesn't like fluffy?

True – true. I don't call myself: "ScaryEvil666SatanicWitchSorceressDarkPriestessofLeviathan", but I sometimes go by the moniker "Adrianna" because that's been my magickal nickname since the late 80's. Of course I've never made my real name a secret, nor the fact that I write fiction AND non-fiction, nor the fact that I have four pen-names. After all, I have to make sure my readers can find my work.

I don't dress in all black. I'm probably not metal. I only have one tattoo. I'm in a stable, monogamous, happy relationship, and have been for 14 years. I have a ::gasp:: career as a novelist. (The occult books are a labor of love.) I spent a large majority of my adult life working in accounting.

I do dye my hair on occasion when I get bored with the natural auburn. I usually go a bit redder. That's probably as wild with my appearance as I get. I no longer smoke. I rarely drink alcohol. I don't do drugs (unless you count caffeine).

My temple isn't covered in black, nor is it full of

Halloween props. Nope – I keep the Halloween decorations in a tote in the basement. I pull them out in October to decorate the exterior of the house for Halloween. The neighborhood kids enjoy it.

I haven't taken any pictures of myself by candlelight, donned in black robes surrounded by Halloween props either.

I don't need to play dress-up to convince others, or myself, who I am or what I am. I know who I am and what I am. I'm rather comfortable in my own skin, thank you very much.

I worship the Daemonic Divine. I practice blood magick. I practice necromancy. I am a priestess. I am a magician. But I don't constantly shout it from the rooftops because I don't have an insecure need to. I'd rather lurk in the shadows of underestimation anyway. It gives me an advantage. I don't end every conversation with blessings of this Daemon or that Daemon or Hail/Ave [insert Daemonic name here].

I don't feel the need to spend all my time trying to convince others that my path is the right one for me, or that I am what I say I am. I have no desire to convert anyone. I have no desire to lead anyone either. You're either called to Daemonolatry or you aren't. That's your business, not mine. I don't spend all my free time trying to invalidate others (or their beliefs) to elevate myself because, believe it or not, I really don't care what complete strangers do or believe.

I write the NF occult books I write because I believe in what I practice and I want to share information with like-minded people. Nothing more, nothing less.

I prefer to spend my time minding my own business instead of everyone else's. This is why I have accomplished so much in my life and have so many published books. I mind my own business and do what I love to do, and I don't really care if others like it or not.

I see so many people out there spending all their time upholding an image, or trying to gather a following, or trying to spread their own personal truths as gospel. This makes me laugh. I wonder how much they could actually accomplish if they put the same amount of effort into bettering themselves and their own lives instead of wasting all that time minding everyone else's business, trying to destroy others, and/or trying to gather a following.

If all of this makes me fluffy, then so be it. I'm fluffy. But at least I'm not a sheep or a poseur.

The Art of Baffling With Bullshit

Pretty sentences are worthless if they only serve to cloak a rather simple principle in mystery, and make it sound more intellectual and complicated than it really is.

I find a lot of limited edition occult books do this these days.

They take 101 material, wrap it in a lot of big words and fancy metaphors, and sell it as 401. This works because, of those people who buy these books now, over 3/4 of them won't be practicing ten years from now anyway. Basically – it's a beginner's market. It always has been when it comes to the occult, and likely always will be. This isn't to say there isn't a market for more advanced material, there is. It's just considerably smaller and publishers print a lot of 101 so they can afford to print the 401. As a publisher and occult author, I have seen this with my own two eyes.

Sadly I can't stand reading a lot of the stuff coming out of the limited edition hardcover market. Some of it is good – yes. But some of it makes me feel like finding the author, smacking him/her upside the head, and sending him/her to a writing class where (s)he can learn how to write concise prose that isn't nearly as dry and meandering.

Okay, in all fairness – these authors can write. They're simply trying to hide that what they're writing is the same shit already out there. They've simply gussied it up in prettier clothes and have sold it as something new and revolutionary. They've taken 2 + 2 = 4, and turned it into a walk in the park where one finds two ducks and two swans swimming in a lake. There's a beautiful sunset and the azaleas are in bloom.

I guess what I'm really saying is, "Get to the point already and quit wasting my time!"

Spending twenty pages listing all the beautiful metaphors you've come up with to describe the sphere of Malkuth is worthless to those of us who have been practicing forever. We get it. Do you have anything new? Revolutionary? Ponder worthy?

Usually the answer is no.

Or perhaps that's what people want. They want books that are really "smart sounding" to bring legitimacy to their practice of magick. I don't know about the rest of you, but I've met authors who write rather concise prose who are very smart sounding. Just because they don't use words like anomalistic, gasconading, and parsimonious throughout their prose doesn't make them less intelligent. It makes them less pompous and not obtuse.

Of course I do see the appeal. I do. It might actually be a fun writing exercise to write something so full of metaphoric nonsense that the reader's eyes glaze over and they say, "Oh yeah! It was really great!" Just because they're pretty sure it was good, but they were so bored they couldn't bring themselves to keep reading. After all – it's called: "A Perspicacious Discourse of Luciferian Thought." That sounds really smart, by-golly.

Don't get me wrong, some of these books are beautifully written. It's like reading an orgy of literary delight for those who love words. For those who are dedicated to a specific Divine Intelligence (Lucifer, Ahriman, Belial, Hekate, etc…) these kinds of books are going to hold the most meaning, and are a testament to the gods within their pages.

But personally, were I to rate such books on a usefulness scale from 1 to 5, I'd say many of them could be a 5 for 101 (if the reader is able to finish it without falling asleep), and maybe a 2 for 401 (if the reader hasn't tossed the book into a fire and cussed the author). Mind you I only give them a two because sometimes there are some interesting and new ideas wrapped up in the ebullient pages of painfully lethargic prose.

Sure – I imagine a lot of folks will say I don't get it. That the genius of these books is lost on someone like me. No, it's not. I get it, I just got it over fifteen years ago – thanks for the pedantic refresher. Even Franz Bardon, as dry reading as he can possibly be, writes with more clarity and less fluff.

For those who love these books – more power to you. I can't waste my time wading through metaphoric cesspools. I have Work to do.

Real Magical Herbalists

Back in the late 90's I ran an online shop I called *Daemonolatry Blends*. I made incenses and oils for customers using mostly herbs from nurseries and companies whose business it was to produce dried herbs. But even then I always grew some of my own ingredients. I've always been one to grow at least some of what I use in my magickal mixtures because I feel including a live element boosts the energy of whatever you're making. I also continually got compliments on my mixtures (never complaints that the oleums felt "dead"). Unlike some producers I know who are purely off-the-shelf herbalists- my "blends" were never "dead" and very rarely did they contain synthetics.

One summer I made a Sitri incense my customers couldn't get enough of made with real Jasmine flowers (picked fresh from my own Jasmine plants). It was heavenly. The oil was just beautiful (and proved to be a great perfume). Needless to say I stopped selling my homemade mixtures because I no longer wanted to do it commercially. It was a lot of work, took a lot of time I didn't have (not with having a job), not to mention I didn't have the ability to grow the live magickal plants necessary for commercial production (Daemonolatry Blends got really busy and popular between 1999 and 2000).

I've always admired herbalists who cultivated some of

their own magical plants. I have even more admiration for the real magical herbalists who grow almost everything they use (or who can find it growing wild and can cultivate it that way). I am fortunate to know a few of these people. I am blessed that they are sharing their knowledge with me when it comes to growing magical plants I haven't grown before. Brid and Val have also given me much better methods for producing synergetic mixtures than what my own teacher taught me. (Sorry to my teacher(s) for the last comment, but I must be honest.)   It's too bad they don't do it commercially because I'm pretty sure their mixtures would become quite popular.

I'm pretty sure that it's not only method by which their blends have more energy. It's the fact that they primarily use plant material from the LIVING plants that they grow (except for special circumstances). When you put magickal intent into something you're growing, when you harvest and dry the plants you can ensure they're both properly infused with the right magickal energy AND fresh. The only synthetics Val and Brid use are oils that are impossible to obtain and the only dried herbs they use from outside suppliers are things they cannot grow themselves.

Having been fortunate enough to be gifted some incenses and oleums from these ladies I can definitely say that these particular mixtures blow most magickal blends out of the water. As a result I have tossed out my entire oleum collection (including five bottles given me by an ex-friend) and replaced them with the better, living versions gifted me. Blends which I'm now learning to make myself.

Now while growing magical plants may not be practical for everyone, being that I'm a working magician I'm beginning to think growing your own magical plants is the only way to control the quality of your own magical blends (not to mention fine tune intent). In my conscience also – it's also the only way to do it if you're selling your magical blends to others and claiming to be some sort of master herbalist.

Real magical herbalists are also, themselves, gardeners. IMHO – real herbalists really know the plants they're working with intimately (in nature!), not just their dead, dried form off a store shelf.

I am enjoying learning about this. Please note I make no claims of being a master herbalist myself. I am not. I'm, at best, merely a magician/alchemist who enjoys gardening, who makes her own magickal blends, grows a lot of her own stuff these days, and has had the privilege of experiencing the difference between incenses and oils made from off the shelf herbs by off-the-shelf herbalists vs. those blends made by people who are actual magical herbalists in the truest sense of the title.

Impressions, Priesthood, & Understanding

I was recently approached by a young man in his twenties who, after telling me he was new to Daemonolatry and his family condemned him for his abilities as a medium, expressed an interest in the priesthood. I went through my classic explanation that unlike most pagan/occult groups (especially online) that we actually required our priests to do a bit of work before they could claim the title Daemonolatry Priest(ess). I also explained, like I do at least fifty times a year, that being a priest only has meaning within the group where you hold that title. It has no meaning outside that group. Just like a Catholic Priest would have no flack in a Jewish Community, a Daemonolatry Priest is only that to the group/people who recognize that title. With this revelation, the young man asked me if I knew of a group he could join.

Luckily he was in a state where there is an active Daemonolatry group, so I put him in contact with the high priest of that group. That particular group is a traditional family sect. After a few days, the priest of the group contacted me asking what I knew about the young man because the young man was telling the priest that he, too, was generational. Basically, the young man gave the priest an entirely different backstory than he gave me. Now he was generational beholden to a different Daemon than the one he told me he was dedicated to, (his new Daemon was one whose sigil he'd asked me for the day before), and he had a family history of Daemonolatry that was never revealed to me during our conversations.

This lead both the priest of the group and myself to think the young man was lying. If he wasn't lying to me, he was lying to my friend. Regardless – he was lying.

I often wonder about the point of such lies. I realize some people are impressed by generational ties in the Daemonolatry community. I'm not one of them. Probably because I have a lot of generational friends and none of them are any different than you or I. They simply had a different upbringing. None of them are any more spiritual or "knowing" than anyone else. The only difference (if they are actually practicing Daemonolaters) is they grew up learning Daemonolatry so they have more knowledge about the religion in general. Just like someone who is Catholic all their lives has more inside knowledge of the practice and worship than someone who just converted. It's the same thing.

I have met generationals who are Daemonolaters in name only and who don't practice. I've even met generational dabblers. Sad, but true. Birth alone doesn't make one an adept or give someone birthright to titles or anything like that. One must still practice.

This young man, like so many into the occult these days, is in a rush to get to the priesthood. They believe the title makes them above reproach. They seem to think it will bring them accolades and respect. That people will immediately treat them as if they're an authority. But none of them want to WORK for it. Earning people's respect and becoming a respected authority is no easy task. Respect is earned and you'll never earn the respect of everyone because not everyone is going to agree with you or feel you deserve your title. There will always be people you are at odds with or have a difference of opinion with. Not to mention – titles are work. Being a priest means you are a good organizer. You can help others. You are a people person.

I laugh because I know so many young folks chomping at the bit to become priests because of the power they think it will give them, while those who truly should be priests either try to avoid the title or bring humility to it. I've recently begun the process of handing my title on to my assisting priestess because I want a different role in our group. I need a role better suited to what my spiritual needs are right now and that role isn't the High Priestess. No, that role is Hekau (which is a Lector Priestess role, but it means I don't have to be in charge anymore.) Being in charge of a group is A LOT of work. It often requires you attend to others more than yourself. It requires you to fret over details and organization and that sometimes takes from your own spiritual practice.

This wasn't the first time I stepped down from my priesthood title. When I was suffering from severe depression, I stepped down from my post for over a year so I could help myself. You can't help others if you can't even help yourself. These young people, however, have no desire to help others. Their want for titles is purely selfish and vain. They want respect and power, not responsibility and humility. Clearly they will lie, like this young man, to get it.

What a sad state our culture is in where, to feel important, people are willing to lie to get titles just to boost their poor self-esteem.

Don't get me wrong. Being the high priestess did teach me a great deal over the years. It did teach me that it's really not all about me. It did teach me humility. But it also taught me a great deal about myself and the nature of deity and energy, and in that knowledge I did become quite powerful.

But lies aren't required to gain that power. Work, on the other hand, is. And titles are often the result of hard work. The hard work doesn't stop with a title either. It simply adds more.

I respect people more if they do the work. I don't care if you have a title or not, and that's the truth. I don't respect a lazy Daemonolater with a title any more than I'd respect a dabbler.

When it is Time to Step Down

There sometimes comes a time when a priest realizes he must step down. This is never an easy decision, but it's one that many of us have faced and it may be a decision you're.

Titles in TG Daemonolatry are often hard-earned, meaning you probably studied hard and put in a great deal of time, work, and commitment to get that title to begin with. As a result it can be difficult to give up, even for a short time. There is such a thing as temporarily stepping down from the priesthood, especially in instances where you cannot give the office the full attention it deserves. You may have decided to step down from your office temporarily to recover from illness or a traumatic situation. Or maybe you've discovered that the office was not one that you wanted to continue with for personal reasons. Whatever your reason, transitioning from priesthood to an adept grade (usually to Adept VII^0 - Adept IX^0) can be jarring and may make you feel like you've lost respect of other members in the group. It may make you feel like all your work was for nothing.

On the contrary, many of us believe that knowing when to step down permanently or temporarily takes a great deal of strength and wisdom. It also takes knowing the self.

There are some very good reasons to temporarily step

down from your position until you are able to effectively lead again. Some of those reasons might include:

- Health Issues (Mental or Physical)
- Family Issues
- Addiction Issues
- Lack of Time to Perform the Necessary Duties

There are also some very good reasons to permanently remove yourself from your priesthood position. Some of those reasons could include:

- Change in beliefs.
- Change in focus (realizing you want to go into a different area of the priesthood or discovering you're not a very good leader)
- Finding the Workload too Large

Remember that your position as a member of the priesthood isn't just about you. It's about other people and in many Daemonolatry groups, the priesthood is the glue that keeps the group together by coordinating meetings, setting up rituals, delegating tasks, disseminating information, guiding others spiritually, or simply listening.

People will still respect you for your knowledge and experience, and if they don't, chances are they never respected you as a priest anyway.

To decide if you need to step down, ask yourself the following questions. How you answer them will ultimately tell you if you should step down or not.

1.   Does staying on mean the group suffers?

2.   Do you really have the time necessary to devote to the group?

3.   Can you realistically run the group in your current state of mind or health?

If you are stepping down temporarily for health or addiction issues, just remember that you are doing the right thing.   It takes courage to step down, confront these things head on, deal with them, then return to your position in a better place health-wise. If you divide your time between group and your health, you're only giving yourself an excuse to ignore one or the other.

A lot of times people will shy away from the decision to step down (even temporarily) because they fear change or loss of status during their time away. This isn't necessarily the case. Many priests have stepped down to take other offices, to retire, or simply to get their life in order before resuming their duties again.   It's your choice to view your situation as an opportunity to find a position you're better suited to, a different group you're more suited to, better health and/or relationships, or you can choose to view it as a disaster. The choice is yours.

Giving up the office will go easier if you are able to take the time to slowly transition out of it by giving your replacement more and more responsibility until you are merely there to offer advice or guidance. This is especially important for older priests who may not be giving up a title, but are instead handing the reins over to a younger priest. A slow transition will help you get used to the idea of no longer being the one to handle all the problems or coordinate all the events.   For many, the idea of handing over a coven that you've labored to build and have spent years cultivating can be a hard thing to let go of. The new leaders may do things differently, and sure, they may not initially do things as well as you could have, but they will learn and grow in their new position just like you did.

Giving up the office will also be easier if you keep reminding yourself that your reasons for stepping down (even if it's just temporary) is for the good of all (including yourself) in the long run. Now not everyone is going to react badly to the decision of stepping down.

For one priest, the idea of stepping down while undergoing cancer treatment is a no brainer, whereas a priest with a substance abuse problem might hang on to their position until the Coven itself rises against the priest and removes him forcibly. Each situation is unique and it's up to each individual clergy member to know him/herself well enough to know when stepping down is selfless or hanging on is selfish.

Some may be wondering if Daemonolatry advocates self-reverence deification, then why would hanging on to a title be bad? Because self-reverence is only useful if you are self-knowing, take self-responsibility, and don't use your ego to harm others. Otherwise you're just egotistical. If you are not able to fulfill your duties as a priest, this is not beneficial to others, thus causing others to resent you.

PRACTICE

Reading and theorizing are great, but I very rarely respect anyone who doesn't actually practice. Putting into practice all the things we learn from our spiritual and magickal practice is where it comes full circle. You either walk the walk or you're just talking the talk. These articles address some of my thoughts on the actual practice of Daemonolatry. Some of these were issues that simply come up over and over again when I'm talking to other practitioners, and the remaining articles come from the musings generated by my own practice.

Magick & the Natural Order of Things

Currently contemplating the relationship between Sia, Hu, Ma'at, and Heka and how it all works together.

This brings up two very pointed lines of questioning:

1. While words are spoken – do they become more concrete when written? Is the written word more sacred? Or do the spoken and written have similar properties power wise? Perhaps different situations warrant the written word whereas others warrant spoken word? Then there are combinations of both written and spoken with which most magick is performed – but often one or the other (or both) are hastily performed. With the spoken word you have the vibrational/tonal/frequency qualities as well. And with the written word you have a deeper contemplation. Each of these provided the magician takes into account and remains mindful of all the different properties of both acts during their planning AND performance. Must experiment with this to see what those differences (if any) are.

2. All actions must be guided by the natural laws of Ma'at. Bringing to light Set causes Horus, Horus Redeems Set. Is this an illustration of Ma'at at work? How does Ma'at come into it with regard to execration magicks? I feel like I'm missing something here – but am on the verge of a revelation. One that will take away that ever-present block in the strength and intensity of the works I send into the universe.

If I'm right – this could have a profound effect on my magickal results in workings from here on out. This will require more refinement in my thought process and thinking — then I need to outline it, form a hypothesis, find a method for testing, and perform the required tests to see if I'm really onto something, or not.

Yes, I suppose this is about ethics to some degree. Or perhaps it's more about working WITHIN the natural order of things instead of against them. Once again, you can swim against the tides of Da'ath, or go with them and see where they lead. This could be another piece of my own Great Work.

About this time someone is going to come along and say – yeah, I read all that in a book. Or even, I wrote about that here… or I already knew that — why don't you? Well knowing is one thing. Truly understanding is another. Each of us has to come to that understanding on our own. Sure – I can read what other magicians who DO understand it wrote. But in reading what they've written — I am merely taking their word for it and not really getting it myself, am I? To truly "get it" you have to live by it and incorporate it into your life in a meaningful and practical way. You have to "*experience*" Ma'at in order to truly appreciate and understand why, how, etc… I've already read the books and numerous essays by other magicians. Now – it's that experience I'm seeking.

Emotional Preparation

I'm convinced a lot of the failure in magick is due to the lack of emotional preparation on the part of the magician. In this I mean that the magician is either ready for the answers or changes the magick is meant to impart, or (s)he isn't.

For example: Perhaps the magician seeks to become wealthy. However, wealth, for many of us, requires a far different mindset than continuing on the current path we may be on.

In instances like this, this is where preparation begins. The magician needs to find not only the willpower to manifest the change, but also needs to deeply analyze his/her self, habits, and emotion about a situation before (s)he seeks to change it.

We've all heard time and time again that it can take numerous tries before one is able to quit smoking or break a bad habit. Perhaps you've been fortunate enough to experience this yourself. That's because those numerous tries cause a person to seek out their real motivations and to find that one thing that will help them change their life for the better. Weight loss works much the same way. People may have to try numerous times before they're able to change the habits that caused them to gain weight to begin with.

Now let's apply this to our example of wealth. Just like it can take many tries to learn how to break a bad habit, it can take us numerous tries to learn how to save money, or make money.

All things worth doing are worth doing well. It's very unlikely that you're going to work magick and suddenly a few billion dollars is going to fall into your lap. Instead, magick often works in more subtle ways by presenting the magus with opportunities. Whether or not you take those opportunities, or can recognize them for the opportunities they are, is part of the process where emotional readiness is imperative.

If your self-esteem lacks, you may not apply for the manager's position that pays more. You may shy away from the suggestion that you publish that book. If you fear failure, you may react the same way to opportunity. Additionally, if you have fear, you may shy away from a more aggressive portfolio, instead going for more conservative investments that won't net as much in the long run. You may find your willpower lacks when it comes to saving money to buy something and hence you always find yourself in debt. There are, literally, hundreds (perhaps even thousands) of reasons wealth magick, and other magicks, may not work for someone and it all starts at that emotional level.

The universe is mental and we do create our own realities.

So the next time you plan magick to manifest anything in your life, give your emotional preparation the same consideration (if not more) as the ritual itself. You may just find a different level of success.

Sacred Words - Sacred Writing

I use a lot of profanity. A lot. I use fuck as a noun, a verb, a pronoun, an adverb and an adjective. I'm also fond of creative profanity like "cock blowing bitch fucker", "twat-knocker", and "cunt-cakes". I also grew up in the family business (male dominated) where I was exposed to profanity daily from an early age. "Naughty" words don't offend me or shock me. However, my study of magick has caused me to give more thought to the words I choose to use — and here's why:

To the ancient Egyptians, words were sacred. Even the mere utterance of certain words was considered either sacred or magickal. They realized that words, whether spoken or written, had power. There was emotion — raw intent — behind words.

In Curses, Hexes & Crossing I discuss "curse words" and how even telling someone to go fuck themselves is, in actuality, a curse.

When you begin to analyze the power of words, you being to realize just how much they shape and mold us. Hurtful words may make us fearful or angry or even introspective or misanthropic. Words can make us sad or bring us joy. Words can conjure such powerful, raw emotions that sway our actions and reactions.

It's too bad we don't always pay heed to our words and the power they have. Especially when spoken in anger. However, that doesn't mean we can't try.

Yes, there are other factors to consider, too. How something is said is just as important as what is said. Tone, expression, body language. All of these things relay intent.

An Experiment:

For just one week, I dare you to try to be mindful of every word that falls from your lips. Think out each response and its potential consequences. How does each thing you say affect those around you? Do you see any patterns emerging? Are you noticing you're always a cheerleader, or always the party-pooper? Are you negative? Remember that moods are contagious and the laws of attraction can be applied to what we say.

Sometimes analyzing what we say, and how we say it, when interacting with others is the first step to discovering how to make small changes in our lives to attract more positivity, abundance, and opportunity.

NOTE: If the first part of this post offended you, I do apologize, but I was going for offensive to prove my point.

So I talked about Sacred Words and Speech. I think it's only fair to discuss sacred writing. If we follow the line of thinking that words have power, that power is amplified when those words are written, carved, or inscribed. The saying "the pen is mightier than the sword" did not come about for no reason, after all.

The ancients realized that by writing something down, or carving it into stone, it had the potential to survive for future generations. From written scrolls made of papyri, to the words carved on temple walls, they knew for certain one thing: writing words down gives them permanence. There is power in permanence.

This is why a lot of rituals ask you to create the seals or symbols, or to write the pacts down by hand. The act of writing something down gives it permanence. It solidifies the intent behind the Work.

This also lends insight into the importance of writing down one's Work in the form of a journal. Yes, you could easily memorize your work, but could you imagine what would have happened if Dee or Crowley had never kept journals? Knowing what we know now about what they wrote down, aren't we happy they did?

While I don't have any meaningful exercises for you this month, keep in mind the power of words and the intent behind everything we write. It's always a good idea to be mindful when possible.

Manifesting Results & Divine Intelligence

When I was initially given the blogging topic for July (Daemonic Manifestation) I honestly didn't know what I was going to write about. Do I talk about theophany rituals? After all, I imagine a lot of people might find the physical manifestation of the Daemonic a fascinating topic. Yes, of course I know of several theophany rituals and no, I don't recommend them. It would be a dire situation that called for such a ritual anyway. Most things can be accomplished quite easily without raising Daemons to physical manifestation.

Then I thought that maybe I could write about a physical manifestation experience (as I have had the experience and I am of the firm belief that anyone who works with the Daemonic long enough will experience a physical manifestation of the Daemonic at least once) but then I don't know that such relaying of experience would serve to do much of anything except entertain. That's kind of one of those things you have to experience for yourself in order to really get it. My personal experiences with the Daemonic, for me, are far more than simple blogging fodder.

Then I read some of the other posts for the month and I thought, "Wow. Everyone got really creative with this topic." Leave it to our sisters in Maine to come up with the post they've got for you. It's a doozy!

So I thought on it some more. That's when it dawned

on me that most Daemonolaters want results whether magickal or spiritual. They want manifested results through the Daemonic Divine. It's the results that matter. I've read a great deal of what other magicians have to say about results and the reasons they give for results that aren't forthcoming as well as reasons why some people get results all the time. I've even skimmed the surface of this topic in some of my own writing.

I think the difference in those who get results from their spiritual work and those who don't is whether or not a person is closed, lazy, or refuses to take self-responsibility as opposed to someone who is open, willing to work, and will accept responsibility for himself. That's the difference between someone who gets a great deal from their spiritual path and someone who doesn't.

Years ago I had a student who would ask me seemingly innocent questions about advanced ritual work I'd done and then never follow-up after I answered her questions. No real discussion ensued. I later was discussing students with another friend, who was also a teacher, who told me about his student. Long story short, it turned out it was the same student and he had been giving her advanced "self-work" to perform and instead of doing the work, the same student had been coming to me asking me about my experiences with certain rituals and then copying and pasting verbatim my experience and submitting it to him as her own work. We know this because we compared the e-mails.

The student didn't want to do the work and was willing to lie. Several years later the student complained that she never got results (spiritual or other) from Daemonolatry or working with the Daemonic and after more than a decade she still felt she needed a teacher. Nothing ever manifested for her. Well, when you copy and paste someone else's results you'll never see any of your own.

So while it's probably cliché the reality is that doing

the work will always manifest results when it comes to working with the Daemonic. Now they may not be the results you want, but I think you'll find they're often the results you need. It's important the practitioner distinguish between wants and needs and recognize they're very different things. One is necessary, the other is not. Most often when we're working magick or we have spiritual goals we have a lot of wants. Sometimes you can't get what you want until you first procure what you need so you can get all your needs sorted out. So it goes.

Open yourself up and allow the Daemonic to manifest in your life. Work with the Daemonic to grow and change into who you need to be. Who you want to be will surely follow. Because the greatest manifestation of the Daemonic is, ultimately, your Self.

Demonic Manifestation & the Brass Vessel

So I wanted to talk about the Brass Vessel, spirit vessels in general, and magick lamps because I think some folks really misunderstand (IMO) what these things are. Clearly a lot of people look at magick lamps and brass vessels and we think of genii. You rub the lamp, the genii trapped in the lamp pops out and gives you three wishes. After that - the genii goes back to his lamp until the next person comes along. The moral of these stories always being, "Be careful what you wish for."

But the fairy tale is far from the actuality. In a lot of ways the brass vessel, some folks like Rufus Opus and Jake Stratton Kent have referred to it as a spirit pot, is very much like a triangle of art in that it's a focal point to bring a spirit or the spirit's influence into the physical realm.

Don't mistake the "spirit pot" - let alone the Grimoiric Magick "Brass Vessel" as anything having to do with Necromancy. I address both Nganga and necromantic "Spirit Pots" briefly in Necromantic Sacraments. That's a different thing. Same concept, different thing.

No, the spirit vessels eluded to in ceremonial magick and the old grimoires from Agrippa to Goetia and beyond are basically open doors for a spirit (usually genii, angelic, planetary, or even elemental) to connect with the practitioner or for their energy to have influence over the practitioner in some way. Yes, it could be said the vessel is a metaphoric "home" for the spirit. That's a very old shamanic idea and really, Western Occultism is really our own shamanic tradition.

And on some level all Western Magicians practice drawing spirit energy through a vessel whether it be an offering bowl on an altar to a specific god, a magickal lamp created to bring forth a certain divine intelligence or spiritual influence, or even a Goetic brass vessel.

In Daemonolatry Goetia I discuss the brass vessel as a sacred place to keep permanent sigil(s) and keep the energy in that (those) sigil(s). Or a sacred space to hold the Daemonic energy itself.

I am no stranger to the brass vessel or the magick lamp. I have a magick lamp on my altar as we speak, and I have a copper vessel in there as well, dedicated to a specific divine intelligence (for whom copper is more pleasing than brass). When I seek out this Daemon's wisdom, I'll approach the vessel and speak to it because it is a gateway to the spirit I'm working with. I tend to construct and deconstruct my vessels as they're needed, depending on the work I'm doing. My vessels have been made from wood to ceramic, to various types of metal. I generally only construct a vessel for long-term work, or at least something I'll be working on for more than a week or two. This is likely the same for most magicians.

As an aside here - I do not generally recommend iron for spirit vessels because iron is grounding and it's magickally considered the heart of the earth. However, Iron is good for opening up the veil and communication with the other side. This is likely why nganga and other types of necromantic spirit pots are made of iron.

Rufus Opus, who has a wonderful blog on magick if

you haven't read it, discusses the brass vessel and "spirit pots" on his blog (do a search). He wrote these posts the summer of 2011. So the idea of "spirit pots" and their grimoiric magick connection is nothing new, clearly.

The issue, for me, comes in where people think they're actually constraining, capturing, or luring (in a sneaky way) a spirit into the vessel. Here's the thing -- the spirit doesn't actually reside in the vessel like the genii in Aladdin's cartoon lamp does. It simply comes through it. This is where myself and other folks tend to differ in our opinions.

Some really believe they're keeping spirits in vessels (either willingly or unwillingly, I've met both types of folks), or that they're capturing spirits with these vessels. This is because they're usually folks who believe a spirit has a physical mass that is somehow finite. Like sticking a genii in a bottle. Or they have really big egos and think they're the shit and that they can control the universe with their special magick. Yeah - I'm a fucking snowflake, too. Aren't we all?

I view it much differently based on my own experience. Since I believe genii, elemental spirits, planetary spirits, Daemonic spirits, god-form spirits etc.... are infinite and have no measurable physical mass, I don't believe you can put a genii in a bottle (literally).

Here's how I think it works -- you put together the materials that resonate with the spirit, these materials are put in the vessel, and this draws the spirit to the vessel. The spirit (its energy and influence) then visits that vessel, being naturally attracted to it by the inclusion of the items within it. The vessel becomes imbued with that spirit's essence or influence, that influence begins to influence (both spiritually and physically) you. Also, meditating over such vessels does generally result in very productive communing sessions with the divine intelligences. Or at least in my experience.

Oh yes, I've tried rubbing my lamps and my vessels (just because you have to say you've at least tried it). I've tried the old grimoiric ways of constraining the Goetic spirits. It simply doesn't work like the mythology tells us. When you're working with the old grimoires you have to have the wisdom to understand what is metaphoric, what is literal, and how to navigate the blinds, often left there to ward off the uninitiated and the casual dabbler.

Once you "get" how it all goes together you understand that "God" (which for me is nothing more than a concept of the All) is no more an affront to Daemons than Daemons are adversarial to "God". All things are simply part of a natural universe working the way it works. Good and evil are perceptions of the magician and we manifest what we perceive. We can take things to a place of light and understanding, or we can take it someplace dark and stagnant. It's a choice.

Thinking you're kidnapping spirits with your powerful magick, and keeping them in vessels (sometimes against their will) to do your bidding, is kind of a creepy choice IMHO. Just sayin'...

Pathwork is Not an Enigma

Not too long ago I was talking to a young man about training for the priesthood. He told me about how he'd gone through the training for priesthood in several other traditions and he was always left feeling like the training had no substance. This left him jumping from tradition to tradition, looking for "the one" that gave him the challenge, depth and structure he so desperately sought.

I wasn't surprised. I see it all the time; students looking down their nose at a curriculum that appears far too simple to be training for an office, role or title.

Now admittedly I can understand this frustration. A lot of traditions simply expect you to perform rituals X, Y, and Z, where you memorize lines and regurgitate them when asked to. It ends up looking and sounding like a bad High School production of Marlowe's Dr. Faustus. They may even make you wait a year in between each of these scripted rituals, too, just to make the title at the end of the "training" a little more difficult to get.

Of course we get out of an education what we put into it. So perhaps the fault isn't in the traditions or their training or their rituals. Perhaps the fault is in the student and their expectations of training for a "higher office".

That's the point in the conversation when I pointed

out to this young man that all rituals and courses of study, especially the important ones leading you to a specific office or title, were all about the path-working.

Sure, you could do any ritual in an hour (or less) and walk away, calling it done. But when you really work a ritual by giving more than a mere two hours of your time, and really commit to working it by pondering and repeating it for months, working it backward and forward, you are path-working.

When you study a book and experiment with the material six ways to Sunday, that's path-working.

That's the difference between just reading a book or doing a ritual, and doing actual path-work.

The old traditions are full of path-work rituals and courses for study cleverly disguised as simple rituals meant to be worked in under an hour and lists of books to be read. But sadly the modern phenomena of the absence of teachers, combined with the instant gratification culture we live in doesn't do a lot to facilitate path-work. Students don't understand it because they don't have a teacher to knowingly shake their head at them, give them a forlorn sigh, and say, "You've missed the point. Go back and do it over and this time, slow down and pay attention."

Path-work actually requires you actually work it. You have to think about the rituals or the material you're studying. You have to follow where your questions, curiosity, and answers lead. This also means you have to question the very core of your beliefs and understand every aspect of every ritual and understand the intent behind every incantation uttered.

Path-work is not this enigma we are lead to believe it is and if you are the spiritual or magickal student you think you are, you'll relish in the path-work and find depth for yourself by understanding that training for an office like the priesthood isn't about just completing a ritual or reading (I've learned the bulk of students merely skim) through a bunch of books.

Instead, it's about actually finding that one thing you missed and focusing on it for a while. Then realizing the next thing and focusing on that until you feel you have mastered the lesson.

Several years ago I embarked on my Path of Ptah. When I initially started the ritual I was viewing it as a "becoming as the creator" or a creative force. It took me a year of doing the ritual over and over again, experimenting with it in different ways, thinking about it, studying it, and living the lessons it was teaching me before I discovered that I had missed the most important lesson of all. I was so busy focusing on the end result that I'd missed the lesson in process. So I took another year and focused on the process.

For those of you who don't know, Ptah isn't a long ritual. It takes about one hour each time it's performed. So sure — I could have done my Path of Ptah in an hour and moved on to my next initiatory rite. But I didn't. Having had the benefit of a teacher who taught me never to do anything in magick half-assed, I worked the ritual until I understood every crack and crevice and element of its design, not to mention all that it could potentially manifest. That little one hour initiatory rite took me two years to complete because I didn't just do a ritual. I did path-work. I've just now moved on to my next "ritual" which I have no doubt I'll path-work that one, too. That is how I do my magickal and self-work because that's how I was taught to do it. Not to mention I feel a deeper connection to my magick through path-work.

So next time you find yourself rolling your eyes at some seemingly simple ritual   or course of study, take a step forward and look a little deeper. Chances are you need to slow down and pay attention because you've probably missed the point.

The Path of Nasa & Alchemical Catharsis

Even within the primordial chaos the cyclic nature of all things rages unchecked. Both cruel and kind, life and death are the subtle transformations and regeneration of all things. Within this chaos is the divine intelligence. The Daemonic forces that rule over all things in creation including those processes that manifest alchemical transformations. In these energies we find Daemons of dissolution, purification, distillation and even putrefaction. Of putrefaction there is Nasa, a Persian-based Daemonic force that rules over all dead matter. This is no small thing. Putrefaction is at work in our lives daily and we can learn a great deal from this process and its ruling Daemonic force, Nasa.

Putrefaction is a process of Saturn and sits beyond the abyss, on the pillar of severity in Binah. In this instance it is also a process that exerts itself most visibly on the material plane. Don't let this fool you. There is a great deal of both mental and spiritual change where putrefaction is at work.

In the past year I donned my alchemist's cap and began growing mandragora officinalis. Mandrake is a Saturn herb and in Daemonolatry it is often used in ascension practice. That is, the practice of ascending to the Daemonic to partake of the wisdom that is divine intelligence. In this instance, the mandrake is taken internally. The leaves are cooling and are not nearly as toxic as the root. Ingesting it has the effect of giving the magician clarity of sight (both visual and empathic) and heightened intuition. Many people report feeling more present and describe their senses as being more vivid when ingesting mandrake tinctures or essences. Please note that this article is in no way suggesting you ingest poisonous plant matter, just pointing out that some people do so for the purposes outlined.

My purpose in sharing all of this will become rather apparent shortly. After growing the mandrake almost a year, I decided to begin tincturing the leaves. Clearly there are several methods to do this. One is to simply cut the fresh leaves from the plant and immerse them in alcohol (usually vodka or rum), or to remove fresh leaves, bruise and cut them, then immerse them into the alcohol. The other method is to create the tincture via a method of putrefaction.

Putrefaction is one of those processes that a lot of magicians don't pay a lot of heed to unless they're fermenting their own home brew. Let's face it, most putrefaction stinks and most people would certainly not want to imbibe it in any shape or form. It was putrefaction that I chose as my method to tincture the mandrake and let me tell you why.

Putting a tincture through the putrefaction process reminds us that even from dead matter, something new is born. We encounter a great deal of dead matter in our lives whether we're clearing our gardens for winter, cleaning out the fridge, moving forward from a dead relationship, or moving on after a loved one dies. Dead matter is dead matter both figuratively and literally.

However, the mandrake leaves put through the putrefaction process don't start dead. Just as dead matters in our lives don't start out dead either. All these things begin as living, vibrant situations or matters with active energy flowing through them. It's when the leaves are cut from the living plant that the putrefaction process begins. Not all the leaves are cut, just one or two. The leaves are then added to distilled water and covered. There, within the darkness of the covered container, the plant matter begins to rot and decompose into the water, its essence absorbed, concentrated, into the water. As the weeks pass, a new leaf is added to the water and more water is added as needed. The plant matter goes from living to dead. This process is repeated for at least one moon cycle. At the completion of the process, all the plant matter has decayed into the water, and the now dead plant matter steeping in the water smells rather unpleasant. Putrid.

This is often how we find dead matter in our own lives. We tend to purposefully cut those living branches that no longer suit our purposes. Some wither, dry up and crumble on their own, but other situations are placed in water as if to preserve them, only for us to come back and discover the matter is most certainly dead and it smells rather unpleasant. However, from the death of a thing comes enlightenment about that thing. Hind sight is, after all, 20/20. This is where Binah, and understanding, in the nature of Saturn, comes in to play.

When you look at a dead situation with new eyes it becomes apparent then that one can now filter out the dead matter while hanging onto the essence of what once existed as a vibrant, living thing. In the putrefaction experiment we simply bottle this essence. We filter the dead plant matter from the now foul smelling water. The once clear water, even after having the matter filtered from it, has now turned a light hue of emerald green. An equal amount of clear alcohol, I prefer Vodka, is added to the liquid to tincture it. The putrid stench subsides and disappears. The essence of the plant is bottled.

In this, perhaps putrefaction is an exercise in letting go of the things that no longer serve us or help us grow. It's an exercise in moving forward and in understanding. These lessons may not always be kind as Saturn can be rather unkind in the lessons it teaches us.

We can still partake of the essence of what was, but in its new, alchemically transmuted form. While a mandrake tincture is taken three drops under the tongue at a time, enjoying a fleeting memory might suffice for our imbibement of our alchemically synthesized life experiences.

Some may choose to purify the dead, but still solid, plant matter by submitting it to the fire. The ash can then be reincorporated into the tincture, or left as white ash (tangible salts), separated. This choice, like every decision we make to leave some things in our past or to carry them with us, is up to each individual.

It is in this we learn the wisdom of Nasa and partake of her. Dead matter(s) should be left to lie fallow. From them comes rebirth from the essence of what once was. In studying putrefaction we are actually studying the process of regeneration.

When my putrefaction experiment was done, my mandrake suddenly began to turn yellow. The leaves withered and died and I was left with a pot containing a root. I patiently watered the barren pot for a month, allowing him to lay fallow, when after a month I noticed green shoots rising again from the soil. The mandrake, while it, itself, does not teach putrefaction, but rather another process of regeneration and the purpose of patience, the purpose of Saturn, the taskmaster planet. Think of Saturn as a strict professor who demands excellence from his students and you'll understand why processes, plants, and even the Qliphothic sphere ruled by this planetary body sit on the pillar severity and force patience, work and processes like putrefaction. Ultimately these things make us stronger, wiser, bolder, and more prepared to face life's many challenges.

If you are not an alchemist or simply have no patience to grow a mandrake and prepare a tincture via the putrefaction process, there are other ways to harness the power of this process. That is to work directly with the Daemon, Nasa. The following ritual can be performed to share in her understanding and the process of leaving behind that which no longer serves you. It is a ritual of putrefaction that will make evident the things that must be left behind, while helping you synthesize and separate the useful essences of the experience.

On a Saturday, on a square of parchment, a piece of wood, or a piece of clay - draw the seal of Nasa. You can heed the planetary hour as well if you so choose.

Notice the alchemical symbolism contained within the sigil itself.

On the opposite side of the seal, draw the fourth pentacle of Saturn. This will draw the planetary influence into the talisman

Carry this with you for one week, in your left pocket for men, or at your left breast for women. If you would like to skip this step, simply feed the talisman a drop of your blood.

Also on a Saturday, open your temple to perform your ritual (based on your preferences), invoking any Daemons or spirits you see fit for The Work, along with Nasa using her Enn:

Akayma eya ana ta Nasa

The serpent wise deals death to lies. Remember this as the enn falls from your lips, its ending hissed. Now, holding the talisman in your hands, visualize the process of putrefaction. A plant decaying in water. Flesh decaying and dissolving. Consequently there are many choices among the death daemonic that would also be suited to this task or would work well paired with Nasa. Now imagine all of these images and thoughts filling the talisman. Close your ritual as you normally would and take your talisman to your bed. Place the talisman beneath your bed for a week. During this time dreams and revelations of those things no longer useful to you will surface and the useful essence will become apparent.

You may also choose to carry the talisman with you. Again, for men in the left pocket, for women at the left breast, but be careful as this may cause more abrupt endings or will serve to sever ties more readily. To put it bluntly, relationships could abruptly end, people could die. Projects can falter. The talisman can be kept wrapped in black cloth in a wooden or clay container, recharged, and reused as you need it, or you may give it back to the earth or the flame so that its power will naturally dissipate and go back to all that is.

Ultimately the Path of Nasa, the path of putrefaction, can be the catalyst for a cathartic event that will bring you rebirth and renewal. Never look upon the death of a thing as a closed door.

Asmodai: An Unholy Trinity

It is said Asmodai derives from the Avestan phrase *aēšma-daēva, meaning "wrath spirit", or as I prefer to say, "Spirit of wrath".   As Asmodeus, he is the Daemon from Talmudic legends, the grand antagonist in the building of the Temple of Solomon, one of the seven Crown Princes of Hell who presides over lust. Allegedly he is a King of Nine Hells in the writings of Renaissance clergymen. In Goetia he is King Asmoday, ruling over legions of Daemonic soldiers. In Goetia he is also Amducius/Amducias, a spirit of musicians and tempests. The name of Asmodeus, like many Daemons, has numerous variants and spellings.

Notice in all of these descriptions that these three Daemonic forces possess the same underlying currents – desire and passion. Desire is the want, whereas passion is the drive to obtain the want.

In Daemonolatry, this is where a different perspective comes into play. We remove all the mythology and look at what these Daemons embody. As it was explained to me during my apprenticeship, three headed, the Asmodai (desires/passions) are Asmoday, Asmodeus, and Amducias. Three aspects of a similar motivating force - each of which is passionate in its own right. Perhaps even wrathful if you could harness the passion behind wrath over the negativity. Passion itself is not negative or positive, it simply is.

113

Asmodeus is sexual desire and passion. Amducias is desire and passion for vengeance/wrath, and perhaps even power. Asmoday is desire and passion for wealth and success.

Asmodai encourages us to explore our desires and find the source of them. To obtain that which we desire. He/it (they) encourages us in our momentum forward toward our goals and that exploration of all of those things we desire. Desire motivates passion. Desire can also be crippling, manifesting jealousy or addiction. Desire drives us to work hard, mate, and build empires. It can also drive us to war. It can help us find companionship or cause us to be forever alone jumping from lover to lover. Without desire, what are we? We are barren. So in that sense, the Daemonic Asmodai forces enrich us and are a path to abundance.

The following ritual meditation will not only help the practitioner connect with the Asmodai current, but also connect with any individual Daemonic force within this most unholy trinity.

Items Need:

- Three red candles inscribed with the following: *Cupiditas Asmodai*

- Anoint the candles with cinnamon and benzoin macerated in grape seed oil.

Now draw the seals of Asmodeus, Amducius, and Asmoday upon parchment. You can use personalized or variant seals of these Daemons.

This ritual is going to be set up in a triangle/pyramid construct. Basically what you'll do here is place one candle over each of the seals in a triangle large enough for you to sit in. The directional placement can be subjective here. I prefer Amducias Southeast, Asmoday North, and Asmodeus Southwest if I'm using the elemental configuration North/Earth, East/Air, South/Fire, and West/Water. If I am putting Water North and Earth West, I will put Asmodeus in the South, Asmoday Northwest and Amducias Northeast. Go with your inspiration and personal associations here. Don't forget to consider alchemical combinations.

Prepare yourself by bathing, drinking a glass of water, and anointing your third eye with flying ointment or the infusion of cinnamon and benzoin. Please be careful and test ALL anointing oils on your leg to make sure you won't have an allergic reaction to it first (before anointing your third eye with anything).

Sit within the triangle nude (or wearing white robes or clothing if you must be clothed), face the south quadrant of the room, and close your eyes. Take a deep breath. Ground and center yourself.

Next, intone the following Enns until your body is vibrating with their essence:

Asmodeus - *Ayer avage Aloren Asmodeus aken*

Amducius/Amdusias - *Denyen valocur avage secore Amdusias*

Asmoday - *Ayer avage Aloren Asmoday aken*

(A Note About Enns: My theory is they're called enns from the alchemical term ens (entia plural). The ens is the influence or principle that affects us. The essence of something. So essentially, the enns (entia) or enn (en) of a Daemon is basically a way to call upon the essence of that Daemonic force. Oftentimes, in communication with a Daemonic force, a magician will receive variant enns attuned to their personal connection to that Daemon, making them most useful to the magician who received them. So if you find yourself compelled to modify the above enns, just go with it and see what happens. Don't forget to write it down.)

Now, when working with Asmodeus, some people report feeling the urge to masturbate during ritual. If this happens it's perfectly normal and the magus should do so if the mood strikes. That exploding release of energy during orgasm can be rather satisfying in a connection ritual like this and can also lend a great deal of energy to any magickal work done in conjunction with this ritual and the Asmodai in general.

For those who enjoy the practice of prayer or oration, the following may be useful and can also be used during targeted operations for manifested results.

Oration for Amducias

Anointed one, bringer of destruction, lord of desolation, lay waste to this which no longer serves me. Make barren the works of those who oppose me. Great Amducias, Lord of the void, bring me vindication.

Oration for Asmodeus

Hail great serpent of lust, Asmodeus, thou art sacred. From the flames arise in want, probing deftly into the depths of the abyss. Arise, arise Daemonic fire, resplendent in the beauty of your invulnerable flame.

Oration for Asmoday

Blessed is Asmoday, bringer of success and wealth to this world. Bestow your abundance upon me that I may live in comfort and dominion the rest of my days.

Oration for the Asmodai

Glory be to the Asmodai, beloved desire, rise within me that I may have great power over all that stands before me. Through you I am master of my life, my world. Hail to the Asmodai.

Next Steps

Now that you have attuned yourself to the current, what do you do with it? You apply it to your goals, of course. Attuning oneself to the desire/passion current is useless unless you plan on applying it. If you don't, you're merely torturing yourself. This is why work with the Asmodai is great for creative types to destroy creative blocks of all sorts. You can most definitely attach your own magickal rites to this one, including scrying so that you may speak with the Asmodai and seek advice in a plethora of matters. From work, to relationships, to spiritual contentment, if there's desire or passion behind it, the Asmodai can be of great benefit.

Modifications

All rituals can be modified to bring the magician his/her desired results. Modification can also be helpful during injury and illness or during periods where a full blown ritual is impractical (such as visiting the Catholic in-laws). This ritual can be done entirely in the astral temple if necessary. Tea lights can be used in place of candles. An incense composed of a pinch of saffron, one teaspoon of cinnamon, one teaspoon of sandalwood, and a half cup of red or yellow rose petals may be burned during this ritual. As this is a fire rite, this work can be done in front of a fire pit with the seals set out in a row next to it. The magician should be facing south in this instance.

Ptah

To become as Ptah is an evocation whereas to bring Ptah (the power of creation) into your life is an invocation.

The Essence of Creation is the Path of Ptah. It is the path all magicians traverse whether they realize it or not. It's the same path artists, musicians, writers, and others who create also travel. It is the path of becoming; of manifestation. Those who create manifest their own will. They create their own realities and destiny.

Real magicians create. It is this creation that is the biggest argument for the modification of magick. Well that and the premise As Above, So Below. After all, if the parameters of all our rituals change depending on the spirits we're evoking or invoking, it stands to reason that rituals also should change from magician to magician to cater to his needs, desires, and individual attributes as well. As Above, So Below.

For what are humans if we are not physical manifestations of the divine?

In the process of becoming is the art of understanding and appreciating the process. It's in that spirit that I am growing magickal plants that require patience and working several alchemical experiments involving my tabletop distillation lab (distillates, obviously). Not to mention

I'll be performing more spagyric experiments this year. I want to bask in the process of Ptah, the becoming. Then I can enjoy the fruits of that manifestation more completely.

I am the embodiment of Ptah resplendent. I am the muse of Atem.

FINIS

This concludes the first volume of *Bound by Blood: Musings of a Daemonolatress.*

NOTES

More from DB Publishing & Official Melissa Press

By S. Connolly

- The Complete Book of Demonolatry
- The Daemonolater's Guide to Daemonic Magick
- The Art of Creative Magick
- Daemonolatry Goetia
- Infernal Colopatiron or Abyssal Angels: Redux
- Curses, Hexes & Crossings: A Magician's Guide to Execration Magick
- Honoring Death: The Arte of Daemonolatry Necromancy
- Necromantic Sacraments
- Kasdeya Rite of Ba'al: Blood Rite of the Fifth Satan
- Nuctemeron Gates
- Abyssal Communion & Rite of Imbibement
- Keys of Ocat (currently published by Nephilim Press)
- Drawing Down Belial

By M. Delaney

- Sanctus Quattuordecim: Daemonolatry Sigil Magick

By E. Purswell

- Goetic Demonolatry

By Martin McGreggor

- Paths to Satan

Various Authors (Compilation Books)

- My Name is Legion: For We Are Many
- Demonolatry Rites
- Ater Votum: Daemonolatry Prayer
- Satanic Clergy Manual
- Ritus Record Libri

Forthcoming from DB Publishing & Official Melissa:

- Wortcunning for Daemonolatry – S. Connolly
- A Witch's Book of Recipes – Brian McKee
- Grimorium Daemonolatrie – S. Connolly & M. Delaney (Melissa)
- Sacrae Infernales – S. Connolly

Workbooks and Journals by S. Connolly

- The Goetia Workbook
- 30 Days of Spirit Work
- The Spirit Workbook
- The Meditation Journal